Diani J. Cosciano 1997

LIVING WITH PROZAC

and Other Selective Serotonin Reuptake Inhibitors (SSRIs)

LIVING WITH PROZAC

and Other Selective Serotonin Reuptake Inhibitors (SSRIs)

Personal Accounts of Life on Antidepressants

edited by Debra Elfenbein

HarperSanFrancisco
A Division of HarperCollins*Publishers*

Living with Prozac and Other Selective Serotonin Reuptake Inhibitors (SSRIs) is presented as a collection of personal accounts. This book does not represent an endorsement or guarantee as to the efficacy of any action, practice, or medication described herein. The individual accounts are not intended to replace or supersede medical consultation or treatment.

Library of Congress Cataloging in Publication Data

Living with Prozac : personal accounts of life on antidepressants / edited by Debra Elfenbein

p. cm.

Includes bibliographical references and index.

ISBN 0-06-251206-4 (pbk.)

1. Fluoxetine—Anecdotes. 2. Depressed persons—Anecdotes. 3. Depression, Mental—Chemotherapy—Anecdotes. I. Elfenbein, Debra.

RC483.5.F55L58 1995

616.85'27'061—dc20 94-49156

CIP

95 96 97 98 99 ❖ RRD(H) 10 9 8 7 6 5 4 3 2 1

This edition is printed on acid-free paper that meets the American National Standards Institute Z39.48 Standard.

Contents

I grasp the hands of those next me, and take my place in the ring to suffer and to work, taught by an instinct, that so shall the dumb abyss be vocal with speech.

—EMERSON

In memory of Lezi, Molly, and Keilin,

and

to the still suffering, may you find your way,

here, among us

Acknowledgments

I want to acknowledge gratefully and copiously the expertise and creative support of Barbara Moulton, Dr. David Cordon, Beth McGowan, David Schechter, Ann Mullen and Karen Graff, Lucy Baruch and Kamala Brush, Siobhan Healey, Susan Rovello, Dr. William Weiss, Lily S. Cohen, Andrée Pagès, Jay, Lee, Phyllis, and Johnny Elfenbein, Margery and Fred Cohen, Carl DeSantis, George Schaeffer, Maribeth Slebodnik and the late Molly, Tracey Messer, Dave Besson, Gwen Besson, Frank Bridges, Barbara Smith, Michele Coffey, Carol Sneath, and the late Joe Hoffner, Ladd Hoover, Marion Weinreb, Rena Schechter, Dr. Peter Kramer, Christopher Aubry and Ana Hernandez, Anne B. Craig, Suzanne Jones, Martha and Marie Silano, Penny Weingarten, Kenny Blums, Stacey Luftig, Karen Kisos, Debby Swayne, Lisa Bach, Lynn Williams, Barbara Palfy, Larry Warren, Gary Peirce, Kelli, the evil Gorsch, and Chris in Edwards Hall on November 12, 1993 (wherever you are, I hope you're learning and reading and enjoying yourself).

I extend my thanks and acknowledgment to the many people who wrote accounts that I was unable to fit into the final manuscript and to those many, many respondents to my ads.

Foreword
by Peter D. Kramer, M.D.

Millions of people are living with Prozac. News reports say that American doctors write more than a million prescriptions for Prozac each month; the number of patients who have ever taken Prozac worldwide—ten million, now twelve, then fifteen—seems to rise as rapidly as the total of "Hamburgers Sold" did on the old McDonald's signs. To these totals must be added millions of prescriptions for similar drugs such as Zoloft and Paxil. The figures of antidepressant usage indicate that we in the developed world are now living intimately with a new technology, a powerful technology that people take into their bodies, their brains, their selves.

Those bodies, brains, and selves respond in diverse ways. We are diverse creatures, in critical ways the most biologically and psychologically heterogeneous species on earth. We are also the most talkative species, and the species most prone to self-examination. Perhaps *Homo sapiens* can be defined as the animal that bears witness. Reflecting in *Listening to Prozac* on my early encounters with patients on the medicine, I wrote: "Prozac was transformative for patients in the way an inspirational minister or high-pressure group therapy can be—it made them want to talk about their experience." Debra Elfenbein's collection of autobiographical vignettes, *Living with Prozac,* is testimony to that phenomenon.

Speaking out are those who got better and those who got worse, often better and worse in dramatic ways—people who have a story to tell. And that is the first observation that anyone looking to this book for guidance should make. The vignettes are not culled from a scientifically selected sample, they do not represent improvement and deterioration in the ratios that occur in practice. The storytellers overrepresent the extremes, as do most aggregations of people impelled to make themselves heard. Much of the value of the book lies in that skewed distribution: readers get a picture of a broad range of effects caused by, or at least attributed to, this new technology.

A few of those effects resemble the "transformations" that were the inspiration for *Listening to Prozac*. Certain patients, on medication, experience not just an amelioration of depression (or of compulsivity, or whatever the acute indication for prescribing may be), but also a change in self-assessment or personality, often a change in the direction of confidence, flexibility, resilience, and assertiveness. These stories raise issues regarding transformation: is the medication altering the self, or unmasking an authentic self that always existed in potential or inhibited form? How it feels to patients varies—to some, the traits feel quite alien.

The difficulty in making sense of that alienation points to a second comment about *Living with Prozac*. As a clinician, I might ascribe a different cause to a phenomenon than a patient does in a self-report. The details are not critical; I mean only to say that the doctor's perspective and the patient's are often quite distinct, and that, except when patients are reporting what their physicians have said, *Living with Prozac* begins and ends with the viewpoint of the patient. This single-mindedness is a weakness of witness or testimony; it is also its greatest strength, especially because the patient's perspective so rarely finds a voice.

Most patients are not transformed. They suffer side effects, they become more agitated or depressed, or they find, to their great relief, that medication ameliorates a painful condition. These are the ordinary consequences of psychopharmacology—except that the last outcome, relief from suffering, is, to take a broader view, quite extraordinary.

For millennia, for the whole of the time that Western authors have dealt with questions of health and illness, doctors have sought to alter consequences of the melancholic temperament. The question often arises whether Prozac and its cousins are miracle drugs. Whether or not, in the past four decades, something amazing has happened in humankind's relationship to melancholy. For this brief span of history, we have been able to affect the physiology of mood through medication in stable and useful ways—not as often as we would like, but frequently and dramatically enough to raise the series of existential questions that pervades the stories collected here, whose theme is choice in how to live with melancholy.

Thus, a third consideration arises concerning witness: the conditions that patients endure before (and too often after) they are medicated entail terrible suffering—pain, confusion, fear, distortions of thought and mood and character. The experience of extremes of mood is likely to impress the reader as much as the experience of response to treatment. And in a culture that stigmatizes difference and glosses over suffering, we are always in need of testimony to the experience of mental anguish.

The testimony here is often eloquent. In part this is a function of what a researcher would call ascertainment bias. With a few exceptions, the respondents are middle-class and middle-aged—most often "knowledge workers": professionals, artists, researchers. These witnesses generally suffer ailments that lead to social withdrawal, like the depression afflicting William Styron in *Darkness Visible*; depression that leads to flamboyant behavior, like Elizabeth Wurtzel's in her memoir *Prozac Nation,* is less in evidence. The perspective is broad but not universal.

The voices we hear are clear and engaging. Often we may want to step in and say, No! Slow down, stop, take care of yourself! Other times we will applaud or be moved by courage. As in the fictional short story, we respond to "voice": there seem to be trustworthy and unreliable narrators. What is remarkable is just how involving these storytellers are, after brief contact.

This anthology is for people taking or contemplating taking antidepressants. Those on medication can gain a sense of where their own experience sits in a spectrum of responses. They will learn something, too, about the range of doctor-patient relationships, the role of psychotherapy alongside medication, and the importance of outspokenness in the face of side effects or bad results.

Those considering taking medication will get a feel for the texture of experience possible in response to antidepressants and of ways that taking medication fits into a life. The reports are unreliable as indications of the frequency of bad responses to medication, nor is the medical information presented always accurate; but even here the incidents recounted can serve as useful taking-off points for discussion with a well-informed clinician. And for those clinicians, these reports have a crucial role. They tell us how we look, and how we fail to look.

Living with Prozac by its mere existence performs a social function. *Listening to Prozac,* though for the most part favorably received, elicited rare but loud squeals of outrage from the medical community—the starched white coat syndrome—because the book had the effrontery to raise with the general public questions not yet settled within the guild. *Living with Prozac* takes a further step in this forbidden direction, fostering discussions by and among patients, entirely outside the medical community. This democratizing of discourse should be empowering and energizing to patients. My hope is that *Living with Prozac*, despite its idiosyncrasies of perspective and to a degree because of them, will have the effect of Prozac and its cousins when they work dramatically: to render the melancholic confident, flexible, resilient, and assertive.

Editor's Introduction

What happens to the body, let alone the mind, when antidepressant drugs are ingested is too often a shock to patients. Patients and their community—families, friends, you, me—need to become educated consumers, need to get what we're paying for. And so to become educated consumers, we share with one another what has happened to us in *Living with Prozac and Other Selective Serotonin Reuptake Inhibitors (SSRIs):* we swallow a pill that frees us to sleep normally; we can concentrate for whole periods of time; we become able to feel and recognize pleasure for the first time, sometimes, in years.

We swallow a pill; it disfigures us—we gain or lose weight, feel bloated, nauseated. We feel jittery or lethargic, above and beyond the symptoms of our condition. We discuss our condition, state our history, and chronicle our disappointments and improvements.

Living with Prozac and Other SSRIs is an anthology of extremely subjective writing. Contributors responded to my search for users of Prozac, Zoloft, and Paxil by mail and telephone. I announced my search in weekly newspapers in cities around the country; in national magazines and professional journals; to colleagues; on Internet; to passing strangers at the height of my enthusiasm.

The purpose of the *Living with* series of books (the second volume is due in 1996; additional volumes are planned—see

Appendix on page 271 for more information) is to present what people experience when using antidepressant drugs or treatment. Each book gathers first-person accounts in a readable paperback format. *Living with Prozac and Other SSRIs* contains neither scientific data nor promotional advertising. It is not a clinical examination of any antidepressants and their effects on a certain population; it is not to be taken as medical research. *Living with Prozac and Other SSRIs* presents subjective accounts on important facets of being on antidepressant medication—from a consumer's point of view.

Prozac, Zoloft, and Paxil—arranged in the order of their introduction to the U.S. market—are new-generation antidepressants that "act by preventing reuptake of serotonin into the presynaptic neuron leading to more serotonin being available in the synaptic cleft."* By specifically preventing the reuptake, or reabsorption, of serotonin, Prozac and the other SSRIs increase the amount of serotonin in the brain. Serotonin is a chemical found within the central nervous system involved in facilitating motor activity and in affecting human behavior.

Prozac, Zoloft, and Paxil reportedly perform as well as the older tricyclic (including unicyclic and heterocyclic) antidepressants but with far fewer side effects. Much has been made of the effect of these three drugs, particularly of Prozac. However, in *Living with Prozac and Other SSRIs* I hope to dispel the simplistic notions that the SSRIs are all good or all dangerous. Unique benefits and difficult side effects abound, from the strengthening of the immune system to the weakening of it, from welcome weight loss to mind-numbing anxiety, from swift improvement of mood to aggravated anorexia.

*Laurence B. Guttmacher, M.D., *Concise Guide to Psychopharmacology and Electroconvulsive Therapy* (Washington, DC: American Psychiatric Press, 1994), p. 62.

Some of the diagnostic uses of the SSRIs are unipolar depression and bipolar depression (also known as manic-depression); dysthymia (low-grade, chronic depression); attention deficit hyperactivity disorder (ADHD); eating disorders, including obesity; panic and anxiety disorders; obsessive-compulsive disorder (OCD); chronic pain; chronic fatigue immune dysfunction syndrome (CFIDS); paraphilia (sexual disorders); ulcers and other gastrointestinal disorders; and seasonal affective disorder (SAD).

Prospective contributors to this book received a set of guidelines, questions designed to structure each person's account within set parameters; a description of the series; and a permission form to sign granting me the right to edit and publish each account. The guidelines are printed in their entirety in the appendix on pages 271–273. Contributors chose to use their real names; real first names with last names' first letter; or pseudonyms. A large majority chose pseudonyms. No announcement that readers may be reading a pseudonymous account will be made, to ensure anonymity. Contributors' home states or regions may have been changed for further protection. Any names that match or resemble the names of real and existing people is coincidence, and no similarity is intentional.

I have tried to honor each contributor's account by altering tone and style *as little as possible*. Nowhere in my editing did I purposely change the substance of an account. I hope each account expresses its contributor's singular nature while being understandable.

There are accounts that discuss more than one drug, including more than one SSRI antidepressant. The placement of such accounts, then, became complicated by contributors' medical histories. I assigned placement based on what the most significant drug is—not necessarily the most positive, however—in a contributor's account. Therefore, if a contributor had tried, for example, Prozac, then Zoloft, and had experienced Zoloft as more influential medication, the account would be placed in the Zoloft section. Throughout the text, all drug names—*except* those of Prozac, Zoloft, and Paxil—are followed by brackets containing the brand or generic names and what the drugs do, for example, BuSpar [generic name: buspirone; antianxiety drug]. Prozac, Zoloft, and Paxil section pages contain each drug's identifying data. A select bibliography and an index of pertinent drug names and effects appear at the end of the book for readers' use.

I remind readers to consult with their own doctors or practitioners rather than make guesses based on any information contained in this book. Remember, each person is unique; what works for a contributor here may not transfer guaranteed success to a reader. In publishing accounts with self-destructive or offensive behavior, I am not condoning or encouraging such painful action. I include them here to illustrate breadth of experience. This book, with its individual contributors, does not represent or speak for any organization or particular group.

As we read in the following pages of lives with all their detail, attitude, and fragility, we must keep in mind our own messy humanity, the better to glean the gifts from the accounts we identify with, even from those by which we might be repelled. I invite you to read and learn.

Debra Elfenbein
Lambertville, New Jersey

PROZAC

[generic name: fluoxetine hydrochloride; selective serotonin reuptake inhibitor (SSRI); second-generation antidepressant with a long half-life (72 hours); therapeutic dose range: 10–80 mg. per day; FDA approved 1987]

Jane Miller, forty-four, lives in Massachusetts.

My primary-care physician prescribed Prozac in August 1993 about two weeks after my husband moved out. He and I had been married for twenty-two years, and his falling in love with a co-worker was such a shock that I couldn't cope. I was constantly crying, not eating or sleeping, feeling suicidal, and obsessing, "Why? Why? Why?"

When my doctor suggested the Prozac, I was open to anything she'd recommend, even heroin, my pain was so intense. I began to take 20 mg. each day. I had no effects for the first twenty days. I worked late hours and weekends; I wrote various assignments; I joined a gym so I could just keep moving. I did anything to head off the pain of this separation.

Three weeks later to the day, I was sitting at my desk at work when I realized I was feeling at *peace.* It was as if my mind had been an ocean—a raging, frothing dark gray mass—but now, almost suddenly, the waves were gently lapping on the beach, and the color was a soft gray-blue. I had not realized what torment I had been feeling before the Prozac calmed it all down. I was awed, and thankful there is something like this drug that helps.

It was as if there now were a space between me and the pain, as if more time than just a few weeks had passed. I could sleep, I could eat. I still felt sad and angry, but now I could put that aside and could be with people without thinking, "They all look so happy, I used to be that way" or "Can they see how miserable I am behind this forced smile?"

A few weeks later I felt a downward turn that wouldn't go away, and spoke with my doctor. She upped my daily dose to 30 mg. That worked very well, almost immediately. Things were on an even keel.

During the winter, I began to date, socialize, have lovers. That's when I noticed that I could not reach orgasm without great difficulty. It was as if I couldn't concentrate, as if I could not pull together my thinking enough to focus on one thing that intently. Before Prozac, it usually took me a long time (ten to twenty minutes) to reach orgasm, even when I masturbated. So this time I tried it on my own, but even with a vibrator it took an hour or more, and at times I even gave up. My sex drive and appetite for sex had not changed at all, just the ability to achieve orgasm.

At this same time, I noticed that I'd forget what I was saying in the middle of saying it—not all the time, but often enough to be a problem. I'd be leading a workshop, something I do frequently, and halfway through a thought, I'd lose the thought and have to ask the participants what I was just saying. I quickly learned how to control that by making my comments much shorter, almost what I'd call "lite" speaking, where I spoke on a surface level rather than with the depth I usually displayed in a workshop.

I have never felt euphoric, "happy" happy, or any other purported sudden personality changes on Prozac. I noticed a general inability to concentrate, to finish something before starting another task. I had to almost say out loud to myself, "No, finish this form before starting on the next one." In some ways my mind was like a horse that I frequently had to rein in to go in the direction I wanted. I did not experience this when driving or reading. But sometimes while cooking, I'd have stop myself from doing every step in the recipe at once. There was this almost frenetic energy.

I also couldn't remember my dreams. I would have a definite feeling that I'd had a dream but could not even begin to retrieve it. This was frustrating to me as a counselor and as a writer. I pay attention to my dreams, and this blank slate was strange to me.

I have also found it hard to lose weight, but I don't know if that's the result of a hysterectomy or not.

In May 1994, on my own, I tapered off to 20 mg. again. I was feeling confident enough to do so. Throughout this time, my ex and I began meeting about getting a divorce and selling the house. Although I was sad and cried after each of these meetings, once I blew my nose I felt, "Okay, that's over, let's get on with things, girl," and I did.

By June 1994, I was actually forgetting to take the Prozac, so by the end of June I did not refill the prescription. I was over the worst of the trauma, I believed. I felt fine.

And I was fine until the second week of July, when everything seemed dark and painful again. I tried to stick it out, but by the end of July realized I was still depressed and, at the urging of my therapist, began 20 mg. of Prozac again. Within three days I felt better. It was not as dramatic a calming down as it was the first time I went on Prozac.

This time around, I am not having the lack of concentration to the same intensity I did the first time around with the Prozac, at least not yet. And I can remember my dreams now, partially because I am trying to and because before I go to sleep, I tell myself I will remember them. They seem no different than my pre-Prozac dreams. But trying to reach orgasm is more monumental an effort than before. I keep telling my new lover that it isn't him. I seem to notice more headaches, but that could be the tension I feel over the divorce and sale of the house.

As of this writing, in September 1994, I am wondering if I should go back to the 30 mg., because 20 mg. just does not seem to be doing it. I am someone who can face pain: I have my own brand of faith, I solve my problems. I face pain because to run away from it only makes pain worse.

But even though I am in a divorce support group and I see a therapist, I still feel down and overwhelmed, as I did before I went to 30 mg. a year ago. All of this is depressing in and of itself: I wonder, will I ever get out of this pain? Is the Prozac extending the pain somehow? Will I ever be able to get off this medication? Can I cope without it?

Maybe these are questions that I'm asking more about the depression than about the Prozac. The two are intertwined. I see my primary-care doctor in a few weeks, and she may up me back to 30 mg. or she may have me try something else, I don't know.

Tom Rolfe lives in Utah.

From the vantage point of my fifty-eight years, a year of regularly scheduled psychotherapy, along with twice-a-year prescription visits to psychiatrists, and seven years of Prozac, Zoloft, BuSpar [generic name: buspirone; antianxiety drug], and Xanax [generic name: alprazolam; antianxiety drug] ingestion, I have some insight into my problem.

I'm a lifelong depressive.

My chemical imbalance is genetic, as indicated by similar depressions in my mother, my brother, and his son. The curse goes on. My twin daughters, now twenty-three, show signs of being depressives also.

As an infant, I'm told, I did not talk, smile, cry, or do much of anything.

As a child, I took care of myself pretty much, with few parental or sibling contacts. I remember feeling lonely. I remember pushing dishes I had dried up next to each other so they would be able to feel each other.

As a teenager, I became a decorous class wit, good student, good "drawer," student government activist, stage performer, and sketch writer. I had friends—a lot of people including teachers knew me—but I always felt I was on the outside of things and of relationships, and spent an inordinate amount of time in solitary, lonely reading.

Having had success in school, being bookish, being entertaining, I became a teacher of history. I was active in teacher-union affairs, including being the president of the local, and was again well known and generally respected by colleagues and students. I also felt like an outsider, doing career-related parlor tricks to pass the time and to show off for attention.

I've experienced three episodes of profound depression—the sort where every waking minute is hellish, with suffocating thoughts of death, disaster, and doom, and physical feelings of an amorphous weight on the flesh, pushing one down into the earth.

During these acute stages, my only desire was to be either dead or asleep. Not having the energy to kill myself, I slept nine or ten hours a night if possible. I would wake with a curse that I was not dead and solace myself that the little death of sleep was only as far off as a nap during the day or long-term sleep at bedtime.

The immediate trigger, or cause, of these three episodes was environmental. In each instance, the black holes sucked me in following the sense of loss I felt at the breakup of a personal relationship. In my late twenties, it was a girlfriend who said good-bye forever. In my mid-forties, it was the death of my last parent, coupled with a very rocky time in my marriage. In my early fifties, my teenage daughters went hormonally berserk, and the loving children they had been mutated into raging monsters who treated my wife and me with hatred, contempt, and indifference.

A loss in each case.

That first episode arrived upon my waking up the morning following the affair's finale. My mental state became the focus of my life and the curse of my life, but I did not seek medical help. The depression's worst stage lasted about a year. The memory of it has lasted permanently. It left me frightened and casually depressed for the next ten years, despite my marriage, the birth of my children, and no serious problems.

The second profound depression, in the early 1980s, came on over a few days' time and lasted about nine months. My wife, who had been suffering intermittently from depression since the birth of the children, was on an antidepressant of the tricyclic sort. I took some of her pills for several days. The side effects were not tolerable: dry mouth, dry everything, constipation so painful I'd have to lie on the floor after a bowel movement, and the feeling I was about to explode from some kind of out-of-control inner energy generator.

Whether the tricyclics would have lifted the depression, I never found out, as I stopped taking them in self-defense. As noted, the depression left on its own anyway.

In the late eighties, the third and worst one settled in over a period of deterioration lasting several weeks. Its cause was my realization that my children were not going to be a source of love anymore. Another loss.

This time, however, I went to a GP [general practitioner] who prescribed Prozac. A few days later I signed up with a psychiatrist and saw him frequently for the next several months. He, too, prescribed Prozac but included BuSpar and Xanax.

I experienced no side effects whatsoever. None. Zilch.

In about five weeks, the depression started to dissipate. By eight weeks, I felt the best I'd felt in the memory of my life. Not manic, just not enervated. Not euphoric, just not sad. Not loquacious, just able to talk fast and accurately when I needed to.

I bought a word processor and began to write, the stuff flowing easily, humorously, from brain to page. My daughters were still raising hell, and I didn't like it, but I no longer took it personally or reacted to their fits with fits of my own.

In the second year of these medications, I stopped taking them gradually to see what would happen. In about six weeks, I felt the slide into physiological depression begin. I resumed their use and have swallowed my allotment each day since.

In 1992, for no particular reason but during the great Prozac scare generated by Ron Hubbard's group, my psychiatrist suggested I replace the Prozac with Zoloft. Maybe it was coincidence, maybe not. Anyway, I had no objection and have been on Zoloft to date, experiencing no difference one way or the other.

In 1991, I got up the nerve to retire from teaching after thirty-one years. I'd been on Prozac, BuSpar, Xanax about three years by then and no longer needed the security of the familiar routine. Since retirement, I've become a stringer for the state's leading newspaper, appearing frequently in print, meeting a lot of people, and gaining a local reputation as being pretty good at my new time-killer hobby.

My children have grown, gone, and become quite decent people again. My wife and I get along without much friction, though she thinks I'm a bit housebound and morbid. And she's right by her lights. I am still a depressive. Never a day without thoughts of the pointlessness of life. Ruminations of how I could kill myself. Hopes that my bladder cancer will recur and kill me. Wishful thinking that my heart will stop while I sleep. Yes, I still love sleep, but it's not excessively sought or attained.

The difference is that the medications—I firmly believe this based on only my own anecdotal evidence—allow me to be depressed only on an intellectual level as I've always been, and not on the profound physiological level that puts one on the floor, curled up and thumb-sucking. Prozac/Zoloft and their helping minions, BuSpar and Xanax, keep me functioning in all ways sans outlandish fears, doubts, inertness.

Happy, I'm not. Never was. Never will be.

But profoundly depressed, I'm not. Probably never will be again—as long as Prozac/Zoloft feed me the chemicals of which I was born in short supply.

Viva Prozac/Zoloft and their successors.

Adele Frances lives in New Jersey, sharing custody of her fifteen-year-old daughter. Her current recipe for staying healthy includes equal devotion to work and play (particularly English folk dancing).

For almost ten years since leaving California and moving to New Jersey with my husband and two daughters, I struggled with depressive episodes, especially during the winter and early spring. I spent endless hours in therapy and eventually went on Desyrel [generic name: trazodone; serotonin agonist], which was very helpful when the depressions became acute.

When my marriage began to fall apart and counseling no longer helped, I came to a terrible crossroads. It was obvious that I could no longer remain married and keep any sense of well-being; it was equally obvious that I had no confidence or ability to exist on my own financially or emotionally. My psyche's solution over the course of fourteen months was to enter into an anxiety-depression that led me to four hospitalizations and one almost-successful suicide attempt.

When the local hospital could no longer help, my psychiatrist suggested I go out of state for long-term hospitalization. In May 1990 I entered Sheppard-Pratt Hospital in Baltimore, Maryland, for three months. It was there I met Prozac.

I had been through many tricyclic antidepressants with little or no success, ECT [electroconvulsive therapy] treatments, intensive talk therapy of all kinds. While feeling much more stable in some areas, I was still in deep despair of ever getting well or having a normal life again. I had been an acutely anxious-depressed person who had lost fifteen pounds (and looked skeletal), was suicidal a good deal of the time, and with little or no control over the negative-obsessive thoughts that ran my life. I had become a calmer but still depressed woman who had no goals, no hope, no ability to get her life on track again within the context of her suburban lifestyle.

When I entered Sheppard-Pratt, I felt it was my last chance to grab at the brass ring of mental health or I would be forever doomed to an institutional life. Life's pleasures—the joy of eating, learning, sexual desire, normal sleep patterns—had all become such a distant part of my past that I could not imagine they would ever be a part of my life again.

During the first two months in the hospital, I was taken off all drugs to get a baseline reading on how I functioned. I journaled viciously every day. Although I was much healthier and more highly functioning than a year earlier, my entries are filled with mood swings—the newly discovered joys of life quickly giving way to moments and days of anxiety and despair—wondering how I'd gotten to this place, fearing I'd never recover.

Therapy was intense and varied—individual and group therapy; art, dance, water, and play therapy—I was therapized ad nauseam. In this safe and supportive environment, I allowed myself to go down to the bottom of my darkness and wrestle with it. It was at this juncture that my doctor suggested Prozac. He calmly explained that it was very helpful to many people, but that there were certain side effects, including anxiety in 11 to 15 percent of the population.

I recoiled in horror. "You're going to prescribe anxiety to me when my own is killing me?" The cure often seems worse than the disease in psychiatric hospitals. I was badly frightened. But the idea of remaining in the hellhole I was in was even more devastating.

So I began Prozac in late July with the warning that it might take four weeks to make any difference, which was discouraging since I didn't see how I could survive that long in my present pain. I was not aware of any difference after starting the 20 mg. dosage, except that I suffered from slight diarrhea. It took me a few weeks to make the association, since I was not warned of this side effect and ascribed it to separate stomach problems.

Therapy continued, and I began to take a more responsible role in the hospital, serving as chairperson for the Patient Activities Committee, and began to make plans for my discharge, which involved moving into a women's boardinghouse in Baltimore and attempting a self-supporting life before returning to New Jersey.

One morning in mid-August I awoke early (my eyes flew open at 6:00 A.M. without fail on Prozac) and noted how my daily awakening was accompanied by less fear and dread, more joy and anticipation, of the day ahead. I decided to try an experiment. I would try to feel afraid and anxious. So I ran through my mind all the anxiety-producing situations I could think of: my relationships with my husband and my estranged teenage daughter, my need to get a job and a place to live, the memories of all my past failures, and my abject fears of remaining sick forever. I played all those tapes, and the most incredible thing happened. I couldn't make myself anxious or afraid! It just wouldn't come. I wrote in my journal, "Now is that Prozac coursing through my system or is it a sign of just-evolving-but-surely-there inner healing and growth? Who knows? Who cares? All I know is I can't bring on the dread!"

From that time I made rapid progress and was discharged Labor Day weekend to begin my three-month stint as a boarder in downtown Baltimore. The Prozac sustained me as I took on work as an office temp, made new friends at the house, renewed my interest in the arts and writing, became actively involved in a nearby church. In short, I greeted each day with the wonder and enthusiasm of a college graduate just off to explore the world.

Despite moments of fear and setback and loneliness, I began to develop confidence that I could manage these feelings. While ongoing therapy girded my efforts, I also had the underlying feeling that Prozac was supporting me in all this. My greatest fear became that some catastrophe would put Eli Lilly out of business and I wouldn't be able to get my precious drug.

One year after going on Prozac, I went off under my doctor's care—as easily as a baby drifting off to sleep. No side effects, no difference in my sense of well-being. By this time I had returned to New Jersey, filed for divorce, begun to establish myself as a women's career counselor for a community college, and fully believed my recovery was more than a medical by-product, but rather the result of long, hard work. However, I still feared I'd miss the Prozac.

My fears were unnecessary. I felt bright and alert and enthused about life after discontinuing it, which gave me even greater confidence that my recovery was now complete. One year later I suffered the loss of a dear friend who had been pivotal in my recovery, and this plunged me very quickly back into a depressive-anxious state. I immediately enlisted my doctor's help, who put me back on the Prozac. Within a month, with the support of friends and professionals and the drug, I was well into recovery. I discontinued the drug within three months to return to my life.

At that point I could not measure whether the drug was truly helpful or if its placebo effect had helped me past the rough spot. It has been my own experience that recovery from unipolar depression is a very subtle interweaving of medication, therapy, and life experience; it's not always possible to discern where one leaves off and another begins.

Prozac seemed to give me steadiness, an inner alertness and brightness, that erased the dread and anxiety of waking up to a totally bleak world each morning. I have now created that same attitude within myself through hard work, good therapy, and a total paradigm shift of how I view myself and the world. But I might never have gotten to this point of independent health and living, had it not been for Prozac at the time I needed it.

Ann Scully, forty-one, lives in the Midwest and works as an addiction therapist.

I began using Prozac in 1992. I had been clean and sober for about four years and began experiencing severe bouts of depression, including an inability to concentrate, loss of appetite, mood swings, and transient suicidal ideation. It became a chore just to get up in the morning to prepare myself for work. I found that I was calling in sick because I was afraid my mood would affect my clients. I discussed my concerns with my therapist, who agreed that a low-dose antidepressant might be helpful.

I saw a psychiatrist who put me on Prozac. He assured me this was the best drug for me because of my history of addictions to cocaine and alcohol. Initially it seemed to be the best. I had some nausea that dissipated after a week and increased sleep disturbances, including not being able to fall asleep and then waking hourly. These disturbances decreased after the first ten days.

I felt like a new person. It became easier to function, and I believe I became a more effective person overall. Things I had not been able to do because of my lack of energy were now again a part of my life. This went on for about a year, when I started having attacks of anxiety and the depression returned.

Even on the Prozac, the depression was worse. I felt bad. My insides were like jelly and the slightest irritation would set me off. I began to wonder if I was losing my mind. I called my psychiatrist, who assured me this was temporary and that things would calm down again. Because I had responded so well to the Prozac initially, he was reluctant to change it.

After enduring six weeks of deepening depression, I took myself off the Prozac. After four weeks off it, I did feel better. I was still depressed, but I wasn't sitting around thinking of ways to kill myself. I also was not isolating myself socially. I did, however, believe that the bottom had dropped out of my life. I endured the symptoms for four months before I decided to seek help again. I did this at the insistence of my therapist. At the time she became adamant about this, she had me sign a no-harm contract. I did go to see a different psychiatrist, one who was certified in addictions and who I knew because I work in the field.

There were some major differences in the psychiatric care I received. This individual actually listened to me and discussed thoroughly the pros and cons of a variety of medications. He wanted to get my sleep cycles regulated and put me on 100 mg. of trazodone [brand name: Desyrel; serotonin agonist] at night. He tried me on Wellbutrin [generic name: bupropion; unicyclic antidepressant] first, assuring me that if it didn't help, we would look at other options. Again, the first month I was on the medication, my mood was optimistic and I began feeling more like myself. I had some anxiety but it was minimal. When the seasons changed, my depression was back, and we discussed the possibility of a seasonal affective disorder rather than just episodic depression.

He increased the Wellbutrin gradually. After four days, I had my first seizure from the medication. He decreased it and finally discontinued it totally because I had an increase in vomiting, headaches, and confusion. I was naturally alarmed by this new set of symptoms, which seemed to be worse than depression. The doctor wanted me to try Effexor [generic name:

venlafaxine; new-generation antidepressant], because it was thought to be helpful for people who had few sustained effects from other medications. At the time of our discussion, however, Effexor was four weeks from being approved by the FDA and not yet on the market. Four weeks later I began taking it.

I am currently taking 100 mg. daily in divided doses and have been for the past two months. I am cautiously optimistic. When I began it, I had nausea, which I still have if I eat after I take it. It seems to be less if I eat first. I initially had some headaches, but they have lessened in both frequency and intensity. I have had no anxiety or other depressive symptoms since I began taking this drug. I also am not experiencing the suicidal ideation. I have felt more able to address in therapy my issues of past abuse and have felt better about myself overall.

When I was depressed, I had no energy to clean out my car or my house. Both those tasks no longer seem so herculean. In addition to my regular job, I have been able to do contract work, which has greatly improved not only my financial status but also my professional standing. I am even doing in-service trainings on addictions for other agencies.

I am acutely aware that the medication is not the whole reason for my changes. I have done a lot of hard work in therapy. For me, the two have gone hand in hand. The medication seems to have helped stabilize my mood, and I am hopeful that this will continue. Sadly, use of an antidepressant, I believe, is a crapshoot. You keep working to find one that works. I am willing to do what I need to in order to avoid the emotional hell I have had to live in.

Andrew Morgan lives in Maryland.

I tapered off a 20 mg. daily dose of Prozac three months ago, after maintaining that level for two years. At one point about a year ago I tried to taper down but decided my life was too complicated to go off Prozac altogether, so I continued the 20 mg. dosage until this complete break.

Has the old me returned to replace the "Prozac me"? Yes and no. There has been a return to a slightly lower energy level than when on Prozac. The work I've done in therapy has enabled me to override the tiredness with clearer thinking and a fresher understanding of being down as part of my creativity. My experience with Prozac has been similar to many of those people described in *Listening to Prozac:* the drug did elevate my energy level, and I was able to relate to others in a more energetic way.

The Prozac me was more vital and consequently could work harder on my marriage and my personal habits of emotional shutdown. Prozac helped me do some new things with myself. It was user-friendly. It was the needed boost to get me to work harder on the real issues of situational depression. If it were not for therapy and an understanding spouse, who also sought therapeutic help for ways to deal with my depression, I would still be reaching for the brown bottle with the green-and-white capsules today.

The situations of my situational depression were these: a divorce, an end to a long-term bridge relationship, and a courtship and marriage to my current spouse of nearly three years; complicated by a diagnosis of cancer and successful surgery two years ago. Underneath all these developments, however, was a long history of unsuccessfully dealing with anger and pain from foggy childhood experiences and some vivid adolescent encounters.

I am astounded to hear of people being prescribed Prozac by doctors who do not insist on a therapeutic context. In my case, a psychologist recommended I consult with a psychiatrist. The psychiatrist, after interviewing me, prescribed the treatment, and I consulted with him several times a year while seeing the psychologist several times a month. Without this network for my personal work, Prozac would have merely afforded me the energy and slightly elevated optimism to blow off my troubles, not address them.

My bottom line? Prozac does have a voice in treating depression. Prozac has helped me start my work of personal change. As I listened to myself while on it, I heard new messages about how well I can do. But those messages only apply to the person I was before the drug came along and to who I am now that I am not reaching for the bottle anymore.

Janet Thacker lives in North Carolina.

I had been seeing a psychotherapist for six months when she suggested that I might need to see a psychiatrist. She suspected that my depression was more than just depression; perhaps it was a chemical imbalance as well. I was totally opposed at first, because a couple of years earlier I had been prescribed amitriptyline [brand names: Elavil, Endep; tricyclic antidepressant]. The side effects of the amitriptyline were terrible for me, so I stopped after four months and then suffered flulike withdrawal symptoms for three weeks. So when my current therapist suggested that I try antidepressants again, I was not receptive. Also, the thought of having to depend on a drug to feel normal was very frightening and embarrassing to me. But as my depression deepened, I reluctantly tried.

My symptoms prior to taking any antidepressant were insomnia, nightmares, loss of appetite, feelings of worthlessness, hopelessness, my relationship with my significant other had fallen apart, lack of concentration, lack of sex drive, and the inability to relate to or get along with others. Coupled with an eating disorder, my problems stem from a history of sexual abuse and neglect as a child, and at some point I have developed a type of chemical depression. By January of 1994 I slept less than two hours each night if at all, ate next to nothing, and was becoming obsessed with suicidal thoughts but in a very removed way. I didn't feel much of anything: I had no desire to go on.

In February of 1994 I saw a psychiatrist and was given a sample of Paxil. I took 10 mg. an hour before bedtime as directed, and began to feel sleepy in about forty-five minutes. I slept only for an hour, then awoke vomiting and suffering from diarrhea, which continued the rest of the night and most of the next day. I never tried it again, and, of course, this experience made me more reluctant to try another type of antidepressant. I decided to try Prozac after much coaxing by my therapist.

I took the first 10 mg. capsule at 9:00 A.M. I did not take it with any food, and my stomach was upset and uncomfortable the better part of the day. I felt jittery, extremely anxious, and had much nervous energy. I found it nearly impossible to sleep for the first couple of months and had to resort to over-the-counter sleeping aids. I had very bizarre dreams when I did sleep. I guess the most powerful side effect of this drug for me was the loss of appetite. Within two months of beginning to take the drug, I lost twenty-five pounds. I had little faith in the drug and none in myself.

I did not follow the directions of my doctor. I skipped doses and took the doses at different times of the day. When I realized how much Prozac controlled my appetite—that I could use it to lose more and more weight—I began doubling and tripling doses to keep from eating. I am not overweight, though my self-image is very poor. I use weight loss and forced vomiting to have control over my body.

Since I did not use Prozac properly, my depression got worse than ever. My therapist explained to me why I felt even worse than before: because I had been so far down, so numb before, that I was not feeling the pain I was in. The little bit of Prozac in the manner I was taking it was bringing me up only slightly, to the level of feeling. So I felt more desperate, more suicidal, and more insane than before I began to take the drug.

My relationship with my partner completely fell apart, I lost my job, tried to kill myself, and was committed to a private mental hospital. I immediately began 40 mg. of Prozac a day; that, coupled with the structure of being in a facility and the counseling, quickly brought me up to a point of managing my own life again.

Since then I still take 40 mg. of Prozac each day. The side effects are minimal; the benefits are numerous. After two months of steadily, correctly taking Prozac, I have been able to sleep without help from other medications. My appetite, though weak, is there and I can stay on a regular diet. The jitteriness and anxiousness I first experienced with Prozac have subsided. As long as I take the medication with at least a glass of milk, my stomach is fine.

My personality has completely reversed. I was so sullen and antisocial before. Now I smile, and I go out of my way to meet people and to make friends. I can concentrate again! I can read a book and do a crossword puzzle from start to finish. I can look to the future now and imagine going back to school, having a career. I have begun to set these wheels in motion, whereas before I could not even see beyond the next day. My relationships with everyone I am close to have altered dramatically, particularly with my life partner. Where everything seemed hopeless between us, there is now lots of hope.

The idea of having to be dependent on Prozac for the rest of my life is still very sad to me, but it helps to look at it in terms of other diseases—I'm like a diabetic who will always need insulin. I don't ever want to go back to the place I was before I began this drug. It has been like opening the dark, dirty windows of my life and allowing myself the fresh air and freedom to be alive!

Jeannette Vanderhoof is in her early forties and lives in upstate New York.

I have lived with depression, its stigma, and its effects for the past seventeen years, from the time I was twenty-six years old and a mother of two young sons. It was not until I was thirty-six that I was actually diagnosed with depression and put on antidepressants.

I remember lying on the couch while my active two-year-old climbed up on counters, getting into everything, practically destroying the house; I didn't care. I couldn't move off that couch. Another incident remains vivid in my memory. I drove to a friend's house for the first time, using her directions. It was dark and I got lost. I called her from a pay phone, sobbing. I totally fell apart. This was so unlike me.

One of the hardest things to deal with was not knowing why I couldn't get control of myself. I began to feel like a failure, a weak person, for not being able to cope. I was very hard on myself, as I'd always been an in-control person, very organized and efficient. I went to doctors, even a psychiatrist, who prescribed antianxiety agents. I was hospitalized twice during that ten-year period, but I never heard the word *depression.* I was diagnosed with stress, anxiety, situational adjustment, etc. At times I seemed to cope well. I had a third child and I went to nursing school and became a registered nurse. But there were periods, at least once a year, when I would become overwhelmed and could not function.

My family doctor started me on tricyclic antidepressants first. I had fairly good results, but bothersome side effects—dry mouth for the first few weeks; lethargy, especially in the morning. I couldn't drive to work without falling asleep at stoplights, and once I woke up just as I was drifting into the opposite lane of traffic. Then in the fall of 1990 my doctor started me on Prozac.

At about the same time some major changes occurred in my life. I had joined a weight-loss group and began to lose a lot of weight. We were experiencing chronic financial problems, and I was questioning my relationship with my husband and separated from him for a short time. My oldest son, nineteen, was involved with a woman ten years older than him, and informed us they were expecting a baby.

I was not monitored very well by my doctor, and I remained on 20 mg. daily until I became severely depressed in May 1991. I had begun to have difficulty working. I wanted to run away, right out of my office. I had difficulty concentrating; I was restless, irritable, and anxious. I had bouts of crying, and I had difficulty relating to my patients (I work with adolescents), becoming frustrated and almost hostile with them. I was seeing a mental-health professional at the time and she arranged for me to be hospitalized. I was put in the care of an exceptional, compassionate psychiatrist, who immediately increased my daily dosage of Prozac and added lithium [brand names: Lithane, Eskalith; mood stabilizer].

Within three weeks I was a new person. I did not experience any side effects at any time. I remember vividly the day the depression lifted. I had gone out on a six-hour pass with my cousin to her home. It was a beautiful spring day. I actually enjoyed myself. I was able to sit and relax in a chair outside instead of having to get up and down and pace, or lie down in bed. After I returned to the hospital I realized I was thinking, "I feel better, I feel good." I actually felt like singing! This was a dramatic recovery for me. Most of my recoveries have been gradual and over longer periods of time.

It was during this hospitalization that my family and I became educated about depression. I was told I had an illness. I needed medication. The brain's chemistry was explained, as well as the neurotransmitters necessary for emotional well-being, and how too much stress can aggravate a chemically unbalanced system. It was an eye-opening experience. I felt so relieved that it wasn't my fault, that I wasn't a weak person who just couldn't cope.

I left the hospital after three and a half weeks with a new, refreshed outlook and a positive attitude. If I took my medicine every day and kept my stress to a minimum, I would be fine. I felt great for three and a half months. I returned to work after being on leave for four months. There was stress in going back to work. There were many questions about where I'd been and what was wrong with me. I became severely depressed quickly and seriously suicidal for the first time. I was hospitalized again and taken off Prozac. My doctor had had experience with other patients becoming immune, so to speak, to Prozac, and he felt it had just stopped working in my case. I spent four weeks in the hospital, finally becoming stabilized on Pamelor [generic name: nortriptyline; tricyclic antidepressant] and lithium. After a few months of this drug regimen, I talked to my physician about going back on Prozac. The times I felt the best were when I was taking Prozac.

I went back on Prozac with my required dosage increased to 80 mg. daily for the best effect. It worked wonderfully for me. Again, I experienced no side effects. I functioned well until the fall of 1993, approximately one and a half years later, when I began to experience subtle signs of trouble. I really did not want to go off the Prozac as I knew it was the best drug for me. My doctor added a low dose of Pamelor, along with the Prozac and lithium, and I improved.

I realize now that for four months I struggled with symptoms of depression and should have recognized that Prozac had probably stopped being effective, as it had once before. I became suddenly severely depressed and within two days made a near-successful suicide attempt. Hospitalized again, I was then started on Effexor [generic name: venlafaxine; new-generation antidepressant], the newest antidepressant, which I am currently taking. It has worked very well. However, I am experiencing loss of sexual desire, which I feel certain is a side effect. This has caused problems for me in my marriage, and I am anxious to try another antidepressant.

Prozac is my medication of choice. I've never felt better than when I was on Prozac, and there are no side effects. However, I now have a healthy respect for the drug. I would like to see myself taking Prozac again, but I would monitor myself very carefully for the first signs of symptoms that perhaps it was no longer effective. My husband is very wary of me ever taking it again; twice he's experienced my rapid decline from healthy functioning to very ill, self-destructive behavior. I'd love nothing more than for my illness to go away and for me never to have to take medication again. That is the hope I have for the future.

Michael Finch is thirty-seven years old and lives in California.

I've suffered from almost constant depression since I contracted encephalitis at the age of seven. The most difficult part of my life was my early school years. I wanted to die. All I knew were humiliation, isolation, and stupidity. I was different from the other kids and quickly became the brunt of their jokes and ridicule. At summer camp or a new school it took only a few days for the new kids to figure me out. My academic performance was poor and I demonstrated little coordination in sports. I had few if any friends. My grandmother caught me hiding in the bushes, secretly watching other children play. When asked why I was hiding, I replied, "Because they might see me."

In high school I began to improve academically and graduated with honors. I was still unable to relate to women, especially sexually. In college I found myself twenty-two years old—the age my parents were when they married—and I had never so much as dated or kissed a girl. I began to write suicide poetry, which my parents discovered. They were shocked by my depression, and I agreed to try counseling. My initial therapist and I thought we saw a manic element in my condition, and I tried lithium carbonate [brand names: Lithane, Eskalith; mood stabilizer] with no effect. I became discouraged and stopped the therapy.

I completed two undergraduate degrees and a master of science degree. I began work as a professional scientist, then rose into management. Years later I tried a new counselor, and I succeeded in forming sexual relations with women after many intensive therapy sessions. I became engaged to a woman I dearly loved. We lived together for several years, then she left me and moved in with another man. Two years later I learned she and her new lover were buying a house similar to the one we had planned. It was then I knew she would never return. I could not go on living. Again, I sought professional help.

I had heard of the controversy surrounding Prozac, which made me eager to try it because I like anything experimental or controversial. I thought that Prozac would not affect me, just as lithium had not. I have a strong psychoactive resistance to most drugs. Much to my surprise, my world began to change two hours after taking the first capsule. Colors appeared brighter; music sounded better; women looked prettier. For the first time I did not want to die. It was as if my world had been skewed and someone adjusted the tracking knob, bringing the horizontal control back to normal. I used to wallow in my agony, even to the extent that I enjoyed the pain. On Prozac I learned that it feels good to feel good.

The only significant side effect (if you can call it one) in the three months I've taken Prozac is an increased sexual libido. My attraction for women is stronger than ever. People say I laugh and smile more than I used to. I have noticed a slight tendency to perspire more than before, but I observe no other side effects.

Prozac does not give me a high or any superpowers. It treats depression by providing a safety net, a basement that I can't fall below. Before, I could fall endlessly down an emotional bottomless pit. Where life once seemed hopeless, now I see possibilities. I'm moving toward those goals, and I can feel the wind in my sails.

Pam Ward lives in Georgia.

Prozac has made a profound difference in my life, but it can only be seen in comparison to my life before I was taking Prozac. I say this because part of my success with Prozac has been the lack of any observable effects from it by others or by myself. People react with incredulity when they discover I take Prozac regularly. I don't feel full of energy or excitable, and I haven't experienced any sleeplessness, none of the side effects of Prozac. It isn't until I go off of Prozac and down into depression that I and others can see a difference.

Early in 1989, when I was thirty years old, my daughter started seeing a child psychologist stemming from complaints of constant headaches for which no physical ailment could be found. My daughter was also regularly going into hysterical fits where she would hit and kick anyone or anything around. The psychologist told me she would have to turn my case over to Children's Services if I did not force my drug-addicted husband to leave. I had a job I hated, with no perceived way out, and large bills to pay that had been run up by my husband. I felt as though I had no control—life was running me and I was hanging on for all I was worth.

When I was depressed, I didn't know I was; I thought I was fine. I was so deep in my little shell, I had no recognition of my own feelings, wants, or desires. I never looked toward the future because it took all my effort just to get through that particular day. I thought little of myself as a separate person, letting my identity consist of components dependent on other people, such as mother, wife, and employee. I had no interest in anything, from eating to caring for my children to taking care of the house. I was constantly listless and withdrawn. I perceived any problem as too overwhelming to be handled successfully. There was a constant, pervading feeling of apathy toward life.

My daughter's psychologist strongly believed in parents being a part of therapy. During the third week of therapy, she took me aside and began to explain the symptoms of depression to me. She said my daughter was probably experiencing slight depression but she felt I was at least mildly depressed, if not moderately. She said my whole countenance showed it. I rarely smiled or showed any emotion, was very quiet and sat with my shoulders hunched over. She suggested I contact my family physician to try to get me on a mild antidepressant for three months to see if it would help me.

I was not convinced I was depressed, but if the doctor thought it might help me I was willing to try almost anything. I started taking 20 mg. of Prozac every morning. For the first week I felt nauseated for an hour after I took it. The first three weeks I was taking Prozac, I felt no real noticeable difference. By the fourth week I began to notice I was able to get out of bed more easily and seemed to have more energy during the day. I started eating more (I had been underweight by about ten pounds) and gaining weight. Work began to seem more tolerable, and I was even beginning to talk to people there. I began to clean my house. I was enjoying my two children more and thinking of them less as a burden.

At that time I did not connect the Prozac to my changes. I had kicked my husband out and begun to learn from the therapist how to raise my children, deal with their problems, and generally be a better parent. I felt medication could not be responsible for my changed demeanor; it was all the positive life changes. So I went off the Prozac about eight months after I started it. It took about two months for the difference to be seen. The difference was seen by close friends and family, not by me. That I could not see a difference is one of the most frightening sides of depression for me. I build a wall to keep all away from me and convince myself my moods are just fine. It wasn't until my family pointed out my symptoms to me and insisted I go back on the Prozac that I did. Within three weeks I was back to my usual undepressed self.

It was an extremely frustrating time for me. I felt I should be able to control my moods myself! There are a number of social factors that contributed to this thinking. The controversy surrounding Prozac made me feel uneasy taking something so many people said was terrible. Then there is the stigma attached to taking a mood-altering drug. People feel you are just too weak to control your emotions yourself. I still have people say, "You don't seem like you would need a drug like that!" These issues, combined with my inability to see any extraordinary changes from the drug, made it very difficult for me to stay on it for any length of time.

Finally, at the urging of my daughter's psychologist, I began short-term therapy to help me expand my understanding of myself and my illness. I was formally diagnosed as dysthymic—having a constant, low to moderate level of depression. Over the next year and a half, weekly therapy coupled with the Prozac forever changed my life. I began to realize the profound difference in myself on Prozac and not depressed, as opposed to the me with an ongoing depression.

Until I began speaking with someone about how I was prior to Prozac and how I am now, I could not see the truly amazing transition that took place. I began to understand I did not have to wait for changes to affect me; I could affect the changes—I was capable of controlling my life and choosing my paths. It was not until the end of my therapy that I began to realize I will have to take Prozac, or some type of antidepressant, for the rest of my life. Now that I understand and can see the difference Prozac has made in my life, I am quite willing to take it.

Now my life is more vastly different than I could ever have dreamed possible five years ago. I've been divorced for four years and am successfully raising two happy, well-adjusted children. I quit working and am currently a full-time student close to getting a bachelor's degree, with plans to go on for my master's. I now look at life with quiet joy and contentment instead of trepidation. I see the future as a series of challenges I'm looking forward to meeting and capable of handling, rather than a long, rigorous journey to be endured.

Edward Roth is a single man who lives on the East Coast.

I was admitted to a hospital complaining of acute gastrointestinal problems, mainly weight loss, constipation, and pain, and I underwent thorough testing in a one-week stay. The gastrointestinal physician who treated me informed me that all tests were negative. From his observation of my behavior and emotional state, he suggested that I might be suffering from depression and referred me to a psychotherapist.

My symptoms of depression and anxiety were quite severe by this time. I felt totally isolated and that there was nothing of value or happiness in my life. I suffered paralyzing panic attacks, apparently for no reason, and it was indeed a chore to live day-to-day, all normal wants and desires having ceased. With no appetite, I lost approximately twenty-five pounds in about eight weeks, and had no sexual desire at all.

In my first visit with the therapist, his diagnosis of severe clinical depression with accompanying panic disorder was immediate, and I was placed on 20 mg. of Prozac, with 3 mg. of Xanax [generic name: alprazolam; antianxiety drug] per day. Within approximately three weeks, I took a turn for the better. Explaining Prozac's effect to my therapist, I could only liken it to a wall in my mind that separated me from my everyday problems, enabling me to face life each day with an increased feeling of well-being. The only side effects I experienced at this time were dry mouth and slight trembling in my hands.

Unfortunately, my story does not end here. It gets much worse before it gets better. Having been in deep denial that my second wife's exit from my life was due to my drinking, the fact now helped convince me that I was an alcoholic. I sought help in the rooms of Alcoholics Anonymous and have been sober and recovering for almost three years.

During the first four months of my recovery, I became euphoric. I was free from alcohol, my life was changing. Giving no heed to my therapist's statement that my depression was due to a chemical imbalance in the brain, I decided to stop taking Prozac and Xanax. I felt I no longer needed them.

Separation, and the inevitable divorce, moving from my house, increasing stress at work, even the loss to my wife of our little dog—living life on life's terms now again began to become unbearable. Depression, the absolute worst in my life, began to set in. I was in the darkest of pits with no hope of escape. I could no longer function. After even going to work became impossible, I met with my therapist and finally told the whole truth about my alcoholism and other problems and concerns I had not let go of. During the next four months I began a very slow recovery.

Prozac did not now seem to work. I tried many other drugs, including Zoloft and several of the cyclic group. I received no relief, and side effects were severe. After missing ten weeks of work and wondering if life was worth living, I found a combination of drugs to begin to provide relief: daily doses of Prozac at 60 mg., Xanax at 8 mg., and Desyrel [generic name: trazodone; serotonin agonist] at 200 mg. Absolutely massive doses. One year later, I have been able to reduce these levels to 40 mg. of Prozac, 3–4 mg. of Xanax, and 100 mg. of Desyrel. I've gained my weight back, plus some. The high level of Prozac prevented any sexual interest, but at 40 mg. this problem is beginning to be helped.

I have discovered a very positive weapon in the fight against depression. Locally there is a support group known as

Depression Anonymous. This group is founded on the Twelve Steps of AA and directed to all people suffering from manic-depression or severe depressive episodes. As in AA and many other Twelve-Step programs, we can relate our problems, symptoms, and feelings to those who have suffered these same things.

Today I have a great measure of peace and serenity in my life. I believe this is a combination of circumstances, medication, activity in the program of AA, and a renewed spiritual awakening.

Dora Houseman is a schoolteacher who lives in upstate New York.

I had always been a fearful and depressed individual. I came from what might be called a classic dysfunctional home—alcoholic father, nervous mother. As the oldest child, most of the responsibility for running the household fell on my shoulders.

I have always had a weight problem, which only continued to grow worse through the years. At the time of my marriage, I weighed about 165 pounds, and by the time I entered therapy my usual weight was around 211 pounds.

I married a man who I had dated for only six weeks, just because he asked me. At that point my self-esteem was so low that I thought I ought to take the first offer I could get. My new husband and I were ill matched, but I became pregnant soon after we were married and my only child, a son, was born three days before our first anniversary. My husband was extremely demanding and took little interest in our child or home.

As a teacher in the New York State public school system, I had five years after receiving my bachelor's to attain my master's degree or I would lose my teaching certificate. Therefore, I worked full-time teaching, raised a newborn, took night classes and summer school, and dealt with a domineering husband. My home was in a constant state of dirt and confusion. I developed stomach ulcers, chewed my fingernails, and smoked two or more packs of cigarettes a day. It seemed as though I had spent my whole life unsuccessfully trying to keep households functioning. The pressures became more and more intolerable, and I finally reached a point where I was considering suicide. It was at this time that I began seeing a therapist.

For the first two or three years after entering therapy, I saw a psychologist on a one-to-one basis. I began to write poetry. Poetry became a great way for me to conceptualize my problems and emotions; some poems were later published in literary magazines. Then I joined a women's support group. Although I was no longer suicidal, my depression did not seem to be dissipating. Shortly after Prozac was released for use by the FDA, the female psychologist who headed my support group suggested I try it.

It took a great deal of convincing to get my physician to write the prescription. He was dubious of the severity of my problems and fearful of the new drug. The therapist spent a great deal of time on the telephone with the doctor before he finally consented.

I began taking 20 mg. each day upon awakening. For the first week or two I felt no particular change. By the third or fourth week I began to feel more euphoric. It was not a manic reaction, more like a lifting of the load. This feeling increased, and by the sixth or seventh week I felt the best I had in my whole life. I was still dealing with the problems at home and work, and sad things still made me sad. The miracle was that good things truly made me happy!

To be honest, I experienced some side effects at that time as well. I had trouble sleeping, and I began grinding my teeth. In addition, my sexual responsiveness, which hadn't been all that good for some time anyway, fell to a new low.

I didn't tell the therapist or doctor about any of this, because everything else was going so well for the first time in my life. My husband noticed the difference in my everyday behavior.

Between my therapy and the Prozac, it seemed that things were improving for us. At that time, he agreed that the sexual problems were worth the trade-off of everything else going so well. My weight went down about ten pounds, and I seemed to have more energy. So my house was looking better, and I began to take an interest in meal preparation and gardening. I also quit smoking.

After a year, however, my husband and I began to fight over my continuing lack of sexual interest. He convinced me to go off the Prozac. After discussing it with the group therapist and doctor, I began taking 20 mg. every other day for six weeks and then ceased taking the drug completely. Things returned to the way they were. Because of my therapy, I continued to exercise some control over my life, but my weight began to go up; my sense of doom increased; and what's more, I wasn't any more interested in having sex with my husband than I had been.

It seemed to me that at least on Prozac everything else in my life was better, so after six months I began taking Prozac again. The marriage eventually ended. The only other concern I had at that time was my writing. I figured I could live without sex and men, but I didn't want to lose my creativity. I hadn't written anything in months. However, this fear turned out to be unfounded. I had to learn to write about different things besides depression, but that was soon remedied. I received a grant from the New York State Council for the Arts to write an educational play, which was produced and toured the four-county school system in which I teach.

It was decided by all parties involved—a new female physician, the group therapist, and me—that I no longer needed therapy but would continue to remain on Prozac. Dealing with divorce and then my son's high-school graduation was as difficult as it has been and will be for thousands of other women in my situation. I was able to deal with these traumas in a unique and creative way. I obtained a two-year teaching position on a Caribbean island and secured a leave of absence from my old job. I should add, however, that if I had needed to resign my longstanding position in order to try this new one, I would have done so. Fear has less and less power in my life.

Before I end this narrative, I would like to discuss the side effects of Prozac I mentioned earlier. All have since passed. I no longer grind my teeth; I sleep soundly through the night; and under loving conditions my sexual desires and ability to function sexually are perfectly normal.

Unfortunately, I also find that I will gain weight as readily as I ever have if I overeat. I do not seem to eat compulsively anymore, and although my nickname will never be Slim, I maintain a weight much nearer normal than ever before.

There has never been a time in my life when I have ever been so happy and optimistic. I believe therapy would have brought me to a point of independence and increased my self-esteem without my taking Prozac; I am firmly convinced that Prozac helped remedy some physical maladjustment, allowing me to experience the joy of life.

Robert K. lives in New England. His principal interests include classical music and literature.

I have been an exhibitionist for most of my sixty-plus years. I have never been arrested, partly because I have been passive in my disorder, but mostly because of dumb luck. By "passive" I mean that, unlike some of my brothers with this disorder, I have not singled out victims but have rather exposed myself in settings where I could be seen by chance.

The behavior began when I was about thirteen or fourteen, and reflected an overriding sense of self-contempt that was my response to years of unrelenting psychological abuse by my father. When I was about seven, a paralytic stroke changed him from a warm and loving parent to an enraged, determined, and skillfully destructive tormentor who devoted the next and final ten years of his life to my humiliation. It was an art form that he perfected over the course of those years.

Despite the damage, I managed to grow up into a perfectly respectable life. I completed college and graduate school; I secured employment and moved ahead professionally. I married and we had children. In my daily work and social life I have been a model of deportment, a conservative gentleman, always neatly and modestly dressed, genuinely polite to women. In my family life in the evenings and on weekends, I was given to long periods of inexplicable anger; I would not speak to my wife or children but would sit in a darkened room in an agony of ill-defined despair, when I was not outside committing my acts of exposure. My wife of course knew that I was ill, but she never knew the dimensions of my illness.

One summer Sunday when I was in my mid-forties, I suddenly and unaccountably became frightened. For the first time I admitted to myself that I was ill. I sought help from a psychiatrist: we worked together on and off for fifteen years, including about four years of psychoanalysis, a process that went very far in reducing my bouts of brooding anger. But again and again, after periods of remission, every spring the exhibitionism would return.

When it would come upon me, I would feel a surge of excitement, as if I had just been freed from the shackles of a conformity imposed on me by a hypocritical society. To a victim of exposure, I might sound unconvincing when I say that the disorder has little if anything to do with sex or even with nudity, at least for men like me. It has a great deal to do with self-destruction, self-humiliation, and self-contempt. When talk therapy did not stop the behavior, I tried going to nude beaches, thinking that this might relieve the pressure, but it didn't work because nudity without the risk of being seen by disapproving eyes did not satisfy.

In the summer of 1993, by chance, I learned of a team of therapists who work specifically with this family of disorders, known as paraphilia. The treatment offered has three components: aversive conditioning, talk sessions (individually or in groups), and the use of antidepressant medication such as Prozac.

Fearful of side effects, I opted at first only for the aversive conditioning and talk therapy. I insisted that depression was no longer a part of my problem. The therapist suggested that I keep a journal of my feelings and thoughts three or four times a day for a while, just jotting down words that came to mind. I did so and was surprised to see the clear pattern that emerged: "despair," "emptiness," "hopelessness," "dear God, when will it end?" What my journal supported was the theory proposed by the therapists, that exhibitionism may be built on a base of dysthymia, or low-level depression. Lifting the depression might quiet the disorder. Desperate, I finally agreed to take a daily dose of Prozac.

For several weeks, I noticed no change at all, but one day I was aware of a silence: it was as if all of my life a radio had been broadcasting static in the living room of my mind, and someone had turned it off at last. Gradually, the urges to act faded as well. I went eight months without feeling the need to expose myself, but as spring arrived I began to have some idle thoughts that concerned me. The therapist increased the dosage, and within a few weeks these thoughts faded as well, and so for the first time in years I went through a springtime without feeling the compulsive need to humiliate myself.

One effect of the medication has been a marked decline in my overall sexual appetite, and frankly I am grateful for that. My compulsive need for sexual gratification had been off the charts, and now is well within a more normal range.

The disappearance of the urges and thoughts (along with the background static) has given me relief from this disorder for the first time in my life. My relationships with my wife and children have improved dramatically, and I look forward to the rest of my years with some hope that I may be free at last.

Roseanne Burch lives in Albany, New York.

Prozac was not my first experience with an antidepressant. When I was eighteen and recovering from a bottle of aspirin, I saw a shrink once in the hospital and once at his office. He wrote a script for me for an antidepressant. Without even looking at it, I crumbled up the script and tossed it in his wastebasket on the way out the door.

A year later, in college, I gave in and tried another doctor who prescribed antidepressants. One pill was not doing any good, so I tried two, three, maybe nine. I ended up in the hospital again, trying to convince the doctors that this was just an allergic reaction, not a deliberate overdose. I almost convinced myself.

I gave up on antidepressants and I gave up on trying to get help for my depression. I just lived with it as I had for as long as I can remember. On and off over the next ten years, I saw a psychologist. I picked a psychologist on purpose because he was not a real doctor and therefore could not give me medications. We worked on my depression only when it became so bad I had no choice. And I let him send me to doctors for medication only when I did not have the strength to fight him anymore. None of the drugs ever seemed to help.

In the early winter of 1989, my sister told me for the first time what our uncle had done to her. I went into shock. Everything made sense and yet nothing made sense. The nightmares were not just nightmares. I was not sick; I was not crazy. He really had molested me, too. When I could not deal with it alone anymore, I started seeing a therapist.

The depression became overwhelming and that is when I started taking Prozac, one a day. I think I must have started feeling a little better. I was ready to tell my boyfriend that I could not see him anymore, that we were just using each other. When he stopped over unexpectedly one night, drunk, I decided this was as good a time as any. But he did not want to hear about it; all he wanted was sex.

My therapist said it was rape, but I still have a hard time calling it that. My depression rapidly became worse, a lot worse. My psychiatrist suggested increasing the Prozac to two a day, taken in the morning so as not to interfere with my sleep. After two weeks, I was starting to feel much better. I was still bothered by many things but I no longer felt so overwhelmed. The nightmares increased almost overnight.

After four weeks I was suicidal, the worst I had ever been in my life. I was very depressed, I could not sleep, and I thought my head was going to explode—the headaches were unbearable. I begged my therapist to help me. With his help, I signed myself into a private psychiatric hospital, where I remained for six weeks. My medication remained the same the entire time, except when I refused to take it.

The headaches consumed me. The psychiatrist insisted that they had nothing to do with the Prozac but had everything to do with the depression, the sexual abuse, the overeating. I believed him because he was the doctor and I was the crazy. The headaches only got worse. I felt like someone had tied a belt around my head and was pulling it tighter and tighter. They gave me Tylenol and aspirin, heating pad and ice, and even tried some nasal spray. Nothing worked. They sent me for a CAT scan, which came out fine.

The depression lifted but the headaches remained. When I was released from the hospital, I continued to see the psychiatrist who had originally prescribed the Prozac. We talked about the headaches. He insisted that they had nothing to do with the Prozac. At a friend's suggestion, I saw a chiropractor. He tried everything he could without any success. After a few months of adjustments, he sent me to a neurologist.

The neurologist could find nothing wrong with me. I asked him, too, about the Prozac. He said that was not it. He prescribed a low dose of another antidepressant to take along with the Prozac. For the first time in about a year, I felt pretty good. I could sleep again, and I was having fewer than one or two headaches a week, instead of almost constantly. After a few months, though, I started to have problems with incontinence, and went to see my regular doctor. She said that the second antidepressant listed incontinence as a potential side effect. So I stopped the second antidepressant and the incontinence went away. The headaches came back.

Even though at least three doctors had told me the Prozac was not causing my headaches, I decided to stop taking it. I did not ask anyone. The depression was not so bad, and so I just stopped.

AND THE HEADACHES WENT AWAY! I spent a year of my life suffering from the worst headaches you can imagine, and then they were gone within two weeks of ending the Prozac. Even with generous health insurance, I had spent a small fortune on drugs, deductibles and co-pays, and the chiropractor. I wanted to sue the private hospital and I wanted to sue those doctors.

I called the two psychiatrists to tell them what happened. The one at the psychiatric hospital never even returned my call, and my then-current doctor said he was mildly surprised, but he just brushed it off, with no apology, with no admission that he made a mistake, with no admission that I was right all along. I suffered needlessly for almost one year. I was hospitalized in part, I believe, because of what the headaches were doing to me.

Prozac did have some positive benefits. I got through the worst episode of depression in my life. I became much more assertive and still am. And I learned to never again take a doctor's word for something that felt so wrong, and obviously was wrong for me.

Now I take Wellbutrin [generic name: bupropion; unicyclic antidepressant] and have been for a few years. It seems to have no side effects. I continue to be much more assertive than I ever was before, but I am not willing to credit anything but hard work for that. I continue to eat too much but nothing like before, and I no longer hate myself for that. I still get depressed now and again. The difference now is that the depression does not last and it never, ever gets half as bad as it used to. And I almost never have headaches.

Lindsay Windsor lives in Pennsylvania with her daughter.

As I write my story, I am still in the throes of a very deep depression. I have been battling this illness since my early twenties; I am now in my early forties. I had a very difficult time growing up being the child of two alcoholic parents. I more or less floundered through those years, trying to stay out of harm's way and always attempting to please those around me.

I joined several support groups after college and also saw a psychiatrist, who prescribed Elavil [generic name: amitriptyline; tricyclic antidepressant] and provided psychotherapy. After waiting what seemed like an eternity for Elavil to bring relief, it finally did and I was able to rejoin the world once again and function in a normal fashion. As the years progressed, though, my depression worsened so much so that, in 1978, my husband had me admitted to a hospital for treatment.

I stayed there three weeks, taking several antidepressants. During my stay, I received several electric shock treatments, which were a truly frightening experience (in those days one was kept awake for them). I left the hospital feeling better but still not well. My husband left me and our fifteen-month-old daughter soon after. I felt relief as I have always preferred to be alone. Those years raising my daughter alone were needless to say challenging financially and emotionally difficult. Reflecting back on those years, I would have to say that I gave up my own life so that my daughter would have a better childhood than mine. She is nearly seventeen now, well-adjusted, and, I believe, a typical teenager.

My severe depression began in 1991 when my mother became seriously ill with throat cancer. Watching her attempt to overcome it with chemotherapy, surgeries, and radiation implants, until there was nothing more to be done for her except the insertion of a stomach tube so that she could simply survive, nearly destroyed me. The inexplicable pain I felt after she died was more than I could bear because I had to be so strong for her during her illness.

I sought the help of a psychiatrist earlier this year when I could no longer live with the pain and hopelessness and had become a complete recluse. He prescribed Elavil on the basis that it had helped me once before. It didn't this time. Actually, I had no side effects either. Because I had great difficulty falling asleep, staying asleep, and waking up too early, he prescribed Desyrel [generic name: trazodone; serotonin agonist]. I continue to take this medication and it has helped my sleeping patterns to improve greatly. Then came my near-fatal experience with Prozac.

My doctor prescribed the usual dose of 20 mg., and I took it just as it was prescribed. In only one week on Prozac, I steadily went downhill to find myself in the most severe, suicidal depression I have ever known. During a follow-up visit with a surgeon (I had had nasal surgery in May), I completely broke down, sobbing hysterically, totally out of control. Upon returning home, I threw some eighty Prozac pills down the toilet. It was either that or I was going to end my life.

I immediately went to see my psychiatrist and told him that taking Prozac was without a doubt my worst nightmare ever. I felt that I was losing my mind. I have never known such confusion, inescapable pain, and suffering. I felt out of touch with reality. After three to four days, I gradually returned to my old self, still depressed but certainly not as severely. Prozac was not for me, ever!

He then prescribed Wellbutrin [generic name: bupropion; unicyclic antidepressant], which I have now been taking for several months. It, too, has not yet had the desired effect. In June, because my depression was still so severe, I was hospitalized for a month, where I received group therapy, art therapy, etc. I also received eight ECT treatments. Upon leaving the hospital, I certainly felt better than I had in years. It was obvious that the ECT treatments were working and they were my answer.

My depression has returned, however, and it appears I will need several more ECT treatments in order for my depression to be lifted. While writing this account, I realized that depression has taken hold of me for half my life. Since medications do not work in my case, and in the case of Prozac, nearly cost me my life, I pray that I will soon find the answer to this unbearable and inescapable pain.

Simon Goodman, thirty-three, plays and teaches music, leads outdoor adventure programs, and enjoys life in Massachusetts.

It was late September, although as a New Yorker amidst the arid desert, I couldn't really tell when I got off the plane. After his friendly greeting, the rehab transport person's first words were, "You look like you just saw a ghost." I might well have been a ghost rather than just seeing one—I felt like an alien on a strange planet, removed from the familiar, lush green landscape of upstate New York and stripped from my familiar yet stifling circle of friends, acquaintances, and doings.

There I was feeling naked and terrified of being found out (which translated in the deepest core of my being to mean inevitable rejection, abandonment, and death). I felt a kind of suicidality without a plan; a vague sense of impending doom and uncertainty that I was going to survive. Later I was to learn that it wasn't living the way I had been living I was afraid of: it was the terror of really feeling the depth of rage, grief, and fear inside, and what life would be like without those feelings surrounding me like a dark, blanketing cloud.

Truth is, I was depressed, though I didn't know it.

I was two years sober and working, I thought diligently, on my recovery from chemical dependency and the codependency resulting from an addictive, abusive childhood. My ego was crushed when my outpatient counselor told me he thought I was getting worse and should give myself the gift of going to an inpatient treatment center.

I had seen the afterglow of others who had returned from treatment and wondered if it would work for me. Even with all my self-doubt, in these past two years I had received some gifts of healing and awakening, some signs of hope and trust in the recovery process. There was (and is) a fighter inside who didn't want to be miserable his whole life. And there was (and is) a little boy who just wanted to be loved and happy. In retrospect, my belief in divine guidance influencing this healing process is affirmed, because I probably would not have been ready for this next step of the journey at an earlier time, say, for instance, immediately after I had stopped drinking.

Prior to arriving at the rehab, I had classic symptoms of depression—depressed mood, chronic anxiety, irritability, sleep disturbance, low productivity at work due to difficulty in concentrating, social isolation. I had built a small circle of recovery buddies and took much better care of myself than I had before sobriety. But I was still unable to maintain a romantic relationship and usually avoided new social situations. I really had trouble enjoying anything or anyone. I tried to look good to the outside world but inside I often felt alone and worthless.

It was Day Three in treatment and the initial evaluation process was almost over.

The doctor asked me, "How long have you been depressed?" Somehow this question triggered a crucial crack in the wall of my denial about my illness. As I tried to recall and define my depression, I was stymied.

After an agonizing pause and with tears streaming down my face, I replied, "I can't remember a time I wasn't depressed."

I was referred to the rehab psychiatrist. When I asked why, he said, "Because you have psychomotor slowing, and you're depressed." The surprise and disbelief on my face at that point could only have been exceeded later during my meeting with the medical director, as he shared his recommendation that I begin taking Prozac.

I was flooded with emotions: shock, outrage, and, underneath it all, shame. I was flooded with attitudes: "How dare they suggest drugs to an addict?" and "I must be really sick (and therefore bad) if he thinks I need medication." Then I began to try to listen to the doctor's careful explanation. I was scared of what this new drug would do to me. And I had my pride. I wanted to recover on my own. What would people say or think when I told them I took antidepressants?

I held on to my skepticism and false pride a few more days, as I lost all appetite, becoming more depressed and anxious. Surprisingly, no one else advised me either way but merely supported me to follow my heart about the decision. The breakthrough came when I was asked by a friend, "How is your way working?"

I started Prozac that afternoon, feeling a mixture of hope and fear. What began as humiliation turned to humility. I surrendered to being open to help—not a blind, uninformed trust in Western doctors and psychopharmacology but rather a sense of spiritual guidance and recovery. I knew full well, as the doctor also carefully reminded me, that I needed to earnestly be engaged with the other elements of treatment; that my pain, anger, and fear wouldn't go away because of a pill.

Prozac made me feel a little weird and spacey but not altered like the illicit drugs I used to take. Both my sleep and appetite improved some. Yet it didn't block my feelings. I still am unsure if the Prozac lifted the clouds so I could let out a lot of pent-up tears and rage, or if it was that I had surrendered at the rehab and had begun opening up in my groups to release years' worth of toxic shame, secrets, and emotional loss. And I'm unsure how much of my lifted heart and spirit at the end of treatment was attributable to a change in neurotransmitters or the result of releasing so much pent-up emotion.

My experience in the rehab was truly a blessing. I continued to take Prozac for three months following my thirty-one days in treatment. During those three months, I followed my aftercare plan (therapy and support groups), resigned from an unsatisfying job and found a different one, and entered a wonderful romantic relationship. I didn't experience any of the symptoms of the pretreatment depression.

I don't recall having any noticeable side effects or aftereffects when I weaned off at the four-month mark. I felt more safe in the world than I ever had, and I was able to experience joy. Again, I struggled to determine if the medication had really made the difference or if it was the rehab treatment that had been so cathartic and heart-opening.

Over the next year some of my symptoms returned gradually—chronic lethargy, difficulty concentrating at work, significant anxiety and conflict in my romantic relationship. I am convinced that the catalyst for these returning symptoms was not biochemical in nature but rather from emotion and memories of old trauma, including incest, that were activated as the romantic relationship grew more and more intimate.

My partner threw "depression" in my face, suggesting that the me she had met nine months earlier was a medicated person and not the real me. Not only did I not believe this to be true but I could see her fears, resentment, and transference being sent my way. I was only on Prozac for the first two months of our relationship, and I didn't notice any changes in mood or behavior after its discontinuation.

Although the relationship dissolved, fortunately, I was able to return to a healing group-therapy process that was very experiential (vs. passive talk therapy). Here I experienced the catharsis and alleviation of depressive symptoms but now without the use of medication. Was my brain generating a higher level of neurotransmitters since I had taken Prozac the previous year? I don't know. What really matters is my quality of life and relationships.

It is now almost six years since I took Prozac. Having changed some deeply held patterns of thinking, feeling, and doing, I now have some tools to deal with the intermittent return of depression. While I don't completely discount the impact of biochemical influences on affect and behavior, I have experienced a holistic healing process that does not rely on an intrusive treatment such as medication.

Today I hear about the controversy about antidepressant medications. I agree with critics who describe their misuse. And I agree with proponents who describe a responsible, integrated use of medication for some people, as one part within an overall recovery plan.

Veronika lives in Missouri.

After two years of intense counseling, I was worse off than when I'd begun. When a doctor told me flatly that I was dying, I decided to check myself into the eating disorder unit of a large city hospital, 130 miles from my small hometown. I was thirty-nine years old. I've been taking an antidepressant since then.

Depression had been my constant companion for about as long as I can remember. The third of five children, I was an intense and sensitive child. The slightest excitement or change in my routine caused sleeplessness. My thoughts raced constantly, dogs chasing their tails. I was constantly being chastised for my inability to concentrate.

My mother suffered from her own bouts with depression and went through extreme mood swings. Finding her unavailable, I withdrew into a fantastic world of self-sufficiency, fueled by books and food. I became a plump child. Although I was not especially heavy, my brothers teased me mercilessly. I concluded that all my unhappiness was surely the result of my weight.

At the age of eleven I began spontaneously to purge food. I loved the clear, clean feeling I experienced after emptying my stomach. The hard knot of pain, both physical and emotional, was temporarily loosened. Initially, it didn't seem to have any effect on my weight. However, during my early twenties, I experienced my first bout with anorexia. I fell in love with the feeling of being thin. It was clean, uncomplicated, and safe. It lasted two years.

The next several years were busy with marriage and family. Although my weight was relatively stable, my emotional life was not. I seemed to lead two lives. One part of me was busy, cheerful, energetic, and talented. On good days I would exhaust myself doing long lists of chores. There was nothing I couldn't do if I set my mind to it. On bad days I felt worthless, withdrawn, and screamed at my kids. I was nonfunctional. I never knew which self would awaken each day, so long-range planning was nearly impossible. I could never integrate my good self with my bad self. I continued to use purging as a way to numb the pain and confusion.

When I turned thirty-seven, I entered a second bout with anorexic behavior. I found a counselor who was determined to save me. We entered into a two-year battle of the wills. The first one who dies, wins, I told myself grimly. I got dangerously thin, just over one hundred pounds.

But something fought to stay alive. I checked myself into the hospital, where I was prescribed the new wonder drug Prozac. Through a controversial procedure called a dexamethasone suppression test, I was diagnosed with a severe chemical imbalance. I was placed on 80 mg. of Prozac per day.

The initial effects were wonderful. My first reaction was, "So this is how the rest of the world feels!" My thoughts began to slow down. The dark clouds that pursued me lifted. I felt serene. I smiled. I began to eat and gain weight, and was released from the hospital after three and a half weeks.

But there were side effects. My mouth was dry, I had trouble sleeping, and I couldn't stop yawning. My limbs kept twitching, and at night I compulsively rubbed my feet together until they hurt. The powerful sex drive I had experienced during my anorectic phase dwindled. I developed a severe case of bronchitis, which I attributed to the medication.

My local doctor prescribed prednisone [brand names: Deltasone, Meticorten; corticosteroid] for the bronchitis, and I began to gain weight at an alarming rate. I surpassed my previous normal weight and soared close to two hundred pounds! I panicked. At the eating disorder unit they had promised me that three sensible meals a day would never cause weight gain.

I decided it was the combination of Prozac and prednisone. I quit taking the prednisone and cut back the Prozac to 20 mg. a day. I cut back on my food intake and exercised frantically, but the weight would not come off. No one seemed to know why I was so overweight, but it surely must be my fault. Had I become a closet eater? I felt angry and betrayed, and began purging again. I managed to lose about twenty pounds, but I knew I would never wear a size six again. Probably not even a size ten or twelve. I stabilized at a size eighteen.

Nevertheless, I continued to eat moderately, take my medication, and go for long walks. My purging became less frequent. Despite the disappointment over my body, my overall mood was still positive. I was determined to grow emotionally and spiritually. There had to be more to life than being thin. I joined a support group and began to meditate. I quit screaming at my kids. I gradually released my need to be perfect. I found wonderful new friendships and renewed old ones.

After a while, I found I could cut the Prozac back to every other day. I found a job I loved, and later decided to finish college. Although I still had trouble with occasional purging, it was gradually getting better.

Over the years I have come closer to accepting my body. I know that appearance isn't everything. In all honesty I have to admit I miss my thin body, but I would rather be known for my integrity and compassion than my dress size. I have reached a comfortable, low-fat level of eating that feels right. I try to ignore the well-meaning friends who tell me that twelve hundred calories guarantees weight loss.

I've tried several times to quit taking medication, under the assumption that sheer willpower would overcome mental imbalance. Each time the gradual and insidious slide into depression warned me that this was not something I could control. I would humbly go back to taking the Prozac.

When 20 mg. no longer kept the dark clouds at bay, I convinced a psychiatrist to prescribe Zoloft. I've been taking 50 mg. a day for about six months. There are few side effects, an occasional twitching and yawning. Mostly I feel balanced. I'm usually able to recognize when I need rest and am able to pace myself better. I graduated magna cum laude with a degree in English education and look forward to a new job.

For now, I've resigned myself to taking medication. I am not seeing a counselor, and see a psychiatrist only for my prescriptions. Although I occasionally grumble about being dependent on a pill, I feel grateful for the medication. With a limited energy level, I go for quality rather than quantity experiences. My eating is moderate and my weight stable. I can't say I will never purge again, but for now I am not doing so. I look forward to an old age filled with joy and wisdom.

Henry Hernandez is a practicing physician in Minnesota.

I am almost forty years old and I've battled depression for most of my life. The earliest I remember was probably fourth grade. I spent my childhood with racial taunts on one side and an abusive, alcoholic stepfather on the other. I was always very sensitive, sometimes overly sensitive. As a teenager, I was the stereotypical geek. Relationships with women frequently ended in devastation. Further, my family moved to Illinois from Arizona when I was twelve, and I found I hated the winters. Years later, I learned my feelings were termed seasonal affective disorder (SAD).

I first thought about suicide when I was fifteen and found a note from a female classmate describing how disgusting she thought I was. I spent the next twenty-three years toying with the idea, feeling I wasn't good enough to exist. There were days when getting out of bed was a major accomplishment, never mind functioning. I felt like this through college, medical school, and my residency.

Functioning in a job was sometimes difficult. I am an obstetrician-gynecologist; we are frequent targets of plaintiffs' attorneys and I lived in constant fear of screwing up and being publicly humiliated in a malpractice suit. Often I used to panic during surgery or a delivery, though most people had no idea how I felt.

I was married to my first wife for eight years, and we had three children together. She couldn't tolerate my depression and became very critical. I, in turn, had many affairs looking for the love and comfort I never had as a child and now didn't have in marriage. We divorced in 1988, and I married someone with whom I had become passionately involved.

I decided to go on Prozac after I discovered my second wife was having an affair with someone. We separated because she owed the air force time and I couldn't go with her because of my kids. Of all my relationships, this one was the most special and the most devastating. I lost thirty-five pounds and wanted to die. I had been considering Prozac for some time, but after feeling I was losing my grip, I went to my internist and got a prescription.

At first there was nothing; then, after three to four weeks, I noticed I was much calmer and I didn't care about things as deeply. My second wife's lover left and she wanted to get back together with me. I found that I could be coldly objective and was not led by the desire to turn back the clock. I chose not to go back and we ultimately divorced.

I started Prozac in mid-1991; I am still taking it. I have never noted any physical side effects. The only effect of which I am aware is a profound indifference and apparent blunting of every emotional response except anger. I am still a very angry person at times, but most of the time I feel numb. Things that used to turn me into a crumpled heap don't affect me anymore. Part of that may be maturity and the wisdom I have gained with years, but I feel much is due to the medication. I tried going off for four weeks and discovered my panic and doubt returning.

My indifference is confusing to me. I can get emotional about things that are distant, like films and books. My kids were talking about the movie *Gettysburg,* oblivious to the significance of either the battle or the speech which Abraham Lincoln gave. I read the Gettysburg Address to them and I cried through it. I think they think I am crazy.

Most of the time, though, I feel like I am much more reserved than I was before starting on the medication. I love my kids and I am close to a few people, but I don't go through the angst anymore. I am more objective, maybe to the point of being cold. I am much more comfortable in social situations and making superficial conversation. I still feel like I'm not all there or that I'm playacting. I am sometimes reminded of David Bowie's character at the end of *The Man Who Fell to Earth* or the psychiatrist's monologue at the end of *Equus.* It may be a sterile existence, but I would rather die than return to the way I was.

Beth, a single mother of an adolescent daughter, lives in San Francisco. Beth is in her senior year of Therapeutic Recreation studies, aspiring to practice art therapy.

In my house the laundry was thrown on the floor only to be picked up and worn again. The cat continued to sleep with me under the covers despite my inability to feed her consistently. I set forth into the world outside to caretake a depleted, dying ninety-two-year-old woman who only knew me as a competent "cheerful sweetheart." My nine-year-old daughter had made her usual trip to another state to spend three months of the summer with her father. I was diving deeply into my fourth year of psychotherapy.

I had completed my research of the elderly woman's heart medication enough to ensure I understood what constituted a lethal dose. This was how I entered my first psychiatric hospitalization.

I was diagnosed with major depression, borderline personality, and post–traumatic stress syndrome. I was told I needed Prozac and that this medication would make me well. I started on 20 mg. daily and was discharged after five days. After leaving the hospital with a week's supply, I had an awakening: I knew nothing about the cost, side effects, or where to obtain my medication. I could not afford the cost of Prozac and my state insurance did not cover it. I was frightened and panicked at not having the one thing my whole recovery depended on. Eventually a psychiatrist cleared Prozac on my insurance and supplied me with prescriptions.

I began experiencing restlessness and anxiety of the agitated type. By the third week I was unable to eat or sleep and had tremors, flashbacks, and constant nightmares. Prozac did two things for me: (1) increased all my depressive symptoms and fed my feelings of failure and hopelessness; (2) gave me enough speed to clean everything a few times over and have energy left to analyze my desperate situation.

During the next three months the intolerable symptoms continued. I had given up on my therapist or psychiatrist responding to my pleas. I decided to do some research and then to see a medical doctor to get help with my symptoms.

Validation and relief came in the form of nortriptyline [brand names: Aventyl, Pamelor; tricyclic antidepressant]. The doctor did explain some of the side effects. I remember him saying that this medicine would help me sleep. After filling the prescription I went home and took two times the prescribed dose so I would sleep well. I remember thinking to myself, "I just want to sleep," and taking a few more pills, but I don't remember taking them all.

Thus I began my second hospitalization. I lived in a residential treatment program for four months while my daughter lived with my angry and confused sister. I refused medication in the beginning, but with my increasing anxiety and panic attacks I caved in to the suggestion of doxepin [brand name: Sinequan; tricyclic antidepressant]. The side effects were very different from Prozac's. I was fatigued, bloated, and constipated, with a dry mouth, only to be visited by a ravenous appetite and constant weeping. I gained forty-five pounds in four months, which fueled my depression, fatigue, and self-hatred.

I left this program and stopped the doxepin. I bought into the theory of pulling myself up by the bootstraps, and I returned home to my daughter, to college, and to the familiar, deadening comfort of lifelong depression.

Nancy Jablonski, twenty-eight, is an attorney living in New Jersey.

This account is written under a pseudonym. I wish I could tell you my name, but doing so would have repercussions on my career. True, I am cured now, but depression carries a huge stigma. Despite all the evidence that it's a medical disease with physical causes, people still think there's something wrong with you. You are, somehow, mentally defective.

In 1985 I had my first depressive episode. It was the winter of my second year of college. There was no Prozac in 1985. The college psychiatrist put me on a combination of Stelazine [generic name: trifluoperazine; antipsychotic drug] and Nardil [generic name: phenelzine; MAOI antidepressant]. These drugs did not cure my depression. They made me numb to the world. During my conscious hours I was a walking zombie. With my mother's help, I struggled through the next nine months. I began weekly therapy with a psychologist. The depression became manageable enough by the fall to allow me to return to college. How I managed to live through those nine months is still a mystery.

But as anyone who has suffered through a depression knows, you're never really normal afterward. Whatever personality factors contributed to the progressive slide from anxiety and nervousness to full-blown depression have to be isolated and reduced. If you recover, the disease has made you a different person. You reinvent yourself. And for the rest of your life, you peer over your shoulder, wondering if some occurrence will trigger another bout of despair.

I started taking Prozac in law school. It was the fall of 1990, and I had become increasingly anxious and depressed during my first semester. By October, I was having daily crying jags and couldn't fall asleep or sleep through the night. I was also suffering other classic symptoms of depression—lack of ability to concentrate, feeling sad and hopeless, and a lack of interest in my favorite activities. Additionally, I was becoming increasingly paranoid about the people around me. Were they watching me? What were they thinking? My therapist suggested Prozac. Because of my experience during college, I hoped the medicine would help me before the depression became debilitating.

I was referred to a psychiatrist who prescribed 20 mg. of Prozac once a day, along with one pill of .5 mg. a day of Klonopin [generic name: clonazepam; antianxiety drug] as a sleep aid. Initially, I took the Klonopin a half hour before bedtime. But because it made me sleep for up to eleven hours at a time, I halved the dose.

After four months I stopped taking Klonopin altogether. Even half a pill made me tired and out of it for the entire day. Plus, the psychiatrist told me that Klonopin was for people having trouble sleeping through the night. After five weeks on Prozac, I could sleep through the night without any assistance.

During my first two weeks on Prozac, I didn't feel any better. I became a bit frantic that it wouldn't work for me. My appetite decreased, compounded by a slight to severe nausea about an hour after taking the drug. When I began taking Prozac at the same time every night and not on an empty stomach, the nausea went away. My lack of desire to eat continued for the first five to seven weeks and I lost about five to ten pounds, which I subsequently regained.

About five to six weeks into treatment, I noticed a marked reduction in my anxiety level. During the semester, I had become withdrawn, an unusual effect since I am an outgoing, extroverted person. After Prozac, I was as talkative as ever. My sense of humor came back and I often joked around. I said things to people I wouldn't dared have said five weeks earlier. Not only did I feel better, I felt powerful, self-confident, and even invincible.

This sense of invincibility worried me. I didn't like feeling larger than life. I asked my psychiatrist if it was possible that Prozac was making me too confident, rather than balanced and normal. He said that this was not a symptom that had been reported with Prozac.

The strangest side effect I experienced with Prozac was existential. During the first few weeks, and less so during the next several months, I felt removed from and outside of my body. I can only compare it to being slightly stoned, without the accompanying lethargy and disorientation. I often felt I was watching myself from the outside, and sometimes couldn't believe that what had happened moments before had actually occurred. I often had to perform a mental check, saying to myself, "This really happened, you must remember it."

The drug's most powerful psychological effect became apparent the first time I went to a movie. It was an almost fearful experience. In the enveloping darkness, I felt as if I had consumed a hallucinogenic drug. The movie seemed to last forever, and I did not remember parts of it afterward. If the colors were very bright, they were too intense, even scary.

Other effects I experienced included terrible flatulence (which subsided slightly with time) and bouts of forgetfulness, especially at night. For example, if I had a phone conversation with someone in the evening, I often repeated the same information to that person the next day. My girlfriends got used to this form of senility and called me Prozac-head.

I stayed on Prozac for the entire first year of law school, took a three-month break from it during the summer, then went back on it at the beginning of my second year when my depressive symptoms reappeared.

I have been taking Prozac, always at the same dosage, for three years now. To this day, I have slight bouts of forgetfulness at night and movies are a strange experience. But I have no nausea, weight loss, nor that weird out-of-body feeling. In my opinion, the body becomes truly accustomed to Prozac only after a year or more of continual use.

Prozac has not transformed my life into one big, happy experience. I still cry when I'm sad, get self-conscious, and when really stressed, I become slightly paranoid. But the drug has allowed me to think and function normally.

Going through a depression is like falling down a well. Just when you think you're about to hit bottom, the bottom drops another thousand meters. And you plummet right along with it.

Prozac does not keep you from falling into the well. But it lets you drop only so far.

Theresa Perfetto is clinical director in Virginia of a program for young adults with emotional disturbances. She enjoys snorkeling, biking, and reading.

I've always been depressed—it's like some annoying sound coming from your car that you can't quite identify, but that you know means something is terribly wrong. Coming from a full-blooded Italian family, I was always told it was my nature to be passionate about everything, and that being loud and emotional was normal. I remember feeling alone, although I always had a lot of friends.

When I was eighteen, I realized I needed help with my lack of motivation to continue on with college, my tendency to isolate, my inability to concentrate when reading for more than ten minutes. Most troublesome, my constant thoughts of suicide were becoming too overwhelming for me. I asked my parents to help me find a therapist. My father was livid that I would go outside the family to discuss my problems, and refused to help me pay for therapy. I went on my own to a local mental-health clinic. The therapist immediately recommended medication, particularly antidepressants. At the time I refused, stating that I didn't need a drug to make me feel better, I had enough problems. Besides, I had tried drugs. After long, agonizing sessions, continued insomnia from night terrors, and the torture of my generally agitated state of mind, I got sick of being with myself and I was finally ready to try anything. I was put on amoxapine [brand name: Asendin; heterocyclic antidepressant] in 1980. What followed? It was a nightmare of nightmares. Dry mouth, constipation, headaches, and for the first week, I slept constantly. It was like being in a fog.

But according to doctors these were normal side effects. After about a month, I had frequent heart palpitations, so I was taken off amoxapine. Thus the beginning of my vegetable-garden variety of on-again-off-again antidepressants. This one was too strong, that one was not good to mix with another one, and so on. Finally, I purchased a *PDR* [*Physicians' Desk Reference*] to navigate my way through the sea of information. Those around me told me they saw a difference. I often wondered if it was worth the price. That is until 1989, when I started with Prozac.

It truly was a miracle drug for me. I felt different after seventy-two hours of taking my first three doses. It was like someone gave me a kick-start each day. I remember saying to my psychiatrist, "So this is what I am supposed to feel like? You mean most people who aren't depressed feel like this?" It was an epiphany.

And the best part of all was that there were no side effects. I was not one of the fortunate ones who lost weight on Prozac. However, I could sleep again. Most people underestimate how wonderful it is to sleep. I don't mean with a sleeping pill or other medication that makes you feel like you've been hit by a truck when you wake up, I mean really sleeping. Almost all my life I was awakened by nightmares or had trouble falling asleep. Much of this also had to do with my distressful past, but I've learned that antidepressants don't drug you—they provide your metabolism with something it is unable to provide enough of itself.

Being the skeptic that I am, I took myself off Prozac a zillion times. Maybe it wasn't the Prozac, I would think; maybe it was just me making progress in my life, me learning how to deal with things better. The same thing would happen each time. I would come off, become incredibly depressed, and have to go right back on again. And in a matter of forty-eight hours, my depression would have lifted. My therapist told me it was because of my denial that I kept taking myself off Prozac. I thought it was my difficulty dealing with reality.

I am currently a psychotherapist myself. Overall, I believe antidepressants are not for everyone. I have seen them work miracles in some and only make others more miserable. Any way you look at it, antidepressants are only another tool to help us reach that place we all strive to reach, only to be happy.

Betsey Jordens is forty years old, married, and living in British Columbia, Canada.

Since 1974 I have had Crohn's disease, a chronic inflammation of the bowel. From diagnosis to 1979 I had little trouble; between 1980 and 1988 I had quite a lot of problems, ending up in the hospital seven times. While this is not abnormal in the course of Crohn's disease, with each flare-up I became demoralized and frightened.

From 1987 on, I felt very much alone with this problem, even though I had excellent medical support and my husband was supremely supportive. My husband and I were running our own book business then, which was a twenty-four-hour occupation. I remember an overall feeling of going around without a layer of skin, as it were.

Everything hurt me emotionally. I would be in the middle of some activity, formerly pleasurable, when I would start to weep for no apparent reason, just an overwhelming sadness. I had no defenses, and everything was just another blow, driving me further under. I know I was suicidal; I couldn't think logically enough to come up with a foolproof method.

In late 1989 I had an intestinal resection done, which left me in the hospital for two weeks. I was off all medication, no more steroids for Crohn's, and I began to feel hopeful as I regained energy and could get around. This good period lasted for a month—it was postoperative euphoria, I guess. Then I could feel myself start to slide back into that hole of depression.

I remember going to sleep at night hoping I wouldn't wake in the morning, really willing myself not to wake, so I wouldn't have to live like this anymore. I should add that when I was severely depressed, little things took on more importance, like having the house just so or doing a task in a certain way, almost in a obsessive-compulsive manner.

I began taking Prozac, 20 mg. per day, in November 1989, from a prescription my family doctor wrote for me while I was on a waiting list to see a psychotherapist. The first side effect was a seasick feeling, being woozy in the head and stomach for the first ten days or so, after which it disappeared. I also had trouble sleeping for the first two weeks.

I had a feeling of reemergence—I began to look forward to things, I had more energy for work, I felt more resilient, the crying spells diminished—so that the better I felt, the more I did, which led to an upward spiral of improved moods and activities.

After six to seven months on a dosage of 20 mg. per day, I felt terrific. I treated myself much better where I had previously been so hard and demanding, the crying spells were gone, and I looked forward to getting up in the morning to see what would come next. Everything seemed to be in context, not bigger than life or exaggerated in importance. I am far less compulsive as far as housework goes. If something doesn't get done today, it will eventually—nothing is that important!

I noticed an increase in my dreams and change in their content. They are extremely vivid and often nightmarish in quality. I was worried at first but now regard them as intriguing rather than upsetting.

Some people would find it disturbing, but the lessening of my interest in sex doesn't bother me particularly, as I was someone with a fairly low-key libido to start with. I think it is a fairly small price to pay for being able to enjoy the many other facets of life.

I began to taper off Prozac two years later, taking 20 mg. every other day, then every third day, then stopping completely. Within six weeks I could feel myself sinking. I was in the process of closing our store, selling our house, and preparing to move. I couldn't get through the move in a less-than-able state, so I went back on Prozac. Within four weeks, I was up and running. The beneficial effects came faster, and the move was accomplished with very little anxiety compared to what I have known previously.

Since then I have been on varying doses of Prozac. The three times I've tried to wean myself off, the same sinking feeling would return, and it would become increasingly difficult for me to get through a day without breaking down. The mood swings were quite scary—it was like having a switch flicked on and off in my brain—especially to those around me, and tiring to go through myself. I have resigned myself to the fact that an antidepressant is necessary for me to function. My only misgivings are the drug's cost (about two dollars per capsule in Canada) and the idea that I may be forever dependent on it—not physically but psychologically.

I feel this drug has returned myself to me, if you can understand that concept. I know my husband found it difficult to live with me in a depressed state, but he has often remarked I have undergone a complete personality change since being on Prozac. I wouldn't say it was complete; I feel like the person I was before I was diagnosed with Crohn's in 1974: bright, interested in everything, active, aware, involved.

Matt Jennings lives in Arkansas.

In the fall of 1992, I bought another car, and though it may seem strange, I consider that purchase to be the beginning of my most recent episode of depression. I have always thought that I like change, but change generally throws me for a loop. In this case, car payments did it. Of course, I did what most people do—I denied what was happening.

After Christmas I first thought it was the usual winter blues I experience, but I seemed to be having problems for quite a while. It was all I could do to get out of bed in the morning and go to work. When I was at work, I had difficulty in concentrating on an issue for very long; it was like having an extended anxiety attack. Sex did not interest me in any way.

I got to where I began to avoid friends and family because I didn't want them to see me in that way. It was a good thing I had two dogs to take care of or I doubt that I would have gotten out of bed on the weekends. I thought that by spring I would be okay.

I have been on antidepressants before, you see, and I didn't want to go back on them because of the dry mouth and the weight gain. So I set out to beat this depression. Having read that exercise helps relieve depression, my first strategy was to join the local fitness club. And I began to work out. Then I really had to push myself hard to go, because I just didn't want to be around people, but I persevered. After four or five weeks I began to realize exercise was not working. When I went to a very close friend at work to explain what was going on, I began to cry in her office. She suggested that I go to my doctor.

I was reluctant to talk to my family doctor about this problem. I feel some people can be helped by therapy, but I believe I have a chemical imbalance. I have been through therapy and have tried the old generation of antidepressants, and did not want to try either method again. Yet my mind understood the pessimism going on, so there was no doubt that it was time for further action.

At the appointment with my doctor, I told him about my symptoms and that I was just not getting pleasure out of life. He was sympathetic and began to ask me questions concerning my level of depression. He did not feel that I should take antidepressants if I was just experiencing difficulties in life. After much discussion, he talked to me about taking Prozac. I was reluctant because of all the articles about people committing suicide and becoming violent. He took the time to talk to me about those issues; because I have known him for a long time and have the utmost trust in him, I agreed to take it. I was truly amazed at the sympathy he and his nurse extended to me during that time and still today.

When I first started with Prozac, I noticed around 10:00 A.M. I would get extremely jittery—as if I had not eaten for hours, even though I already had had breakfast. When I was at a convenience store to get something to eat or drink, I would be pretty embarrassed because my hands would shake when money was exchanged. I talked to my doctor and nurse about this; they asked if I felt I could continue to try it for a couple more weeks. I am glad they suggested that or I am not sure if we could have nipped this depression episode in the bud.

Another thing I noticed was that I was constipated a lot. However, I changed my diet and that is no longer a problem for me. There also seemed to be a problem with my memory being short, but I took care of that by making lists, and so today that is not much of an issue. These side effects were acceptable because I didn't have a dry mouth like with the old antidepressants.

My mood began to improve, I could concentrate, and work began to seem enjoyable, instead of the way to make the mortgage payment. My energy level returned, and I was wanting to go around people again. My obsessive-compulsive nature was under control, and I could juggle more things at once without feeling like I was falling apart. In general, I was back in balance and, in the words of a lot of people, I am myself again!

When I would call my doctor for another thirty-day supply of Prozac, I found myself at times downplaying how good I was feeling for fear that the doctor would take me off it. Sometimes I would get a chill through my scalp—and I would think, "This is great!"

I risked a lot to tell a lot of my friends and family how good I was doing on Prozac, that I was no longer ashamed of the depression. I just hope if other people are having problems, they would know they do not have to go through months of suffering. I told one relative and he said, "Matt, you're stronger than that." In my depression this would have devastated me, but I realized that he just could not understand like some of my other friends. I smiled and went about my business. One of my co-workers asked me one day if I had taken my happy pill. At the time it just seemed an odd comment, and I dismissed it. Some people seem to have the misconception that people taking Prozac are always up. For me, that is not the case. I still feel the highs and lows of life, and when I need to cry, I do it. Before, I held a lot of emotions inside.

Mid-winter, I began to feel depression slipping in again, even though I was still taking Prozac once a day. Needless to say, I was saddened by this turn of events. I called my doctor to have him take me off of the medicine; he set up an appointment for me to come in. When I got to the appointment, I wanted to increase my dosage. It must have seemed to the doctor that I could not make up my mind about what I wanted to do.

He began to probe my conflicting phone call and what I was saying in his office. I finally told him that the dosage was not working and I wanted to either go off Prozac or increase my dosage, because as it was, it was not helping. He increased my dosage to two a day and I have been doing great ever since. Again, I began to feel better. I noticed increased self-confidence, hopefulness, and interest in a passion I had left behind in my mid-twenties: my music. I also have become the vice-president of a statewide organization of my peers and seem to be doing something every weekend.

My sex drive returned to what I consider to be normal for me. I was taking care of my car again and keeping it clean. Yes, I have gained weight, but in my case I was underweight when I first saw my doctor. Most people are now saying I look healthier. I am eating more fruits and vegetables than before.

It seems that depression runs on both sides of my family. There are those such as my mother who try to fight it rather than go on medication. I will not go through that again. Perhaps it is a generational issue, but I knew something wasn't right and I have been on a quest to get things right, even though I suffered almost six months before I went to the doctor. My doctor and I have now discussed the possibility that I may have to take Prozac for the rest of my life. If that is the case, I have no problem with it. I hope to one day go off of Prozac to see what happens, but I can assure you that if I have further depression, I will be back on it as soon as possible. I am not ashamed.

Gloria Sherwood lives in Washington.

My first suicidal depression developed when I was fourteen years old. I was too afraid and did not trust anyone to discuss my suicidal thoughts. I strongly believe that I became suicidal due to the fact that both my parents were emotionally abusive to me and that my dad had raped me quite often during my first sixteen years of life; in addition, he had beaten me several times. I have two brothers and three sisters who will support my claims, because not only did they witness me getting abused, they were abused as well.

Even when I was sixteen and, finally with the help of my sisters, told the police on my dad and he was removed from our lives (thank God), the authorities did not send me to a psychiatrist. I wish they had, but at the time my mom wouldn't allow it, and the child-protection laws were different in the early 1970s.

So because of all that, I didn't get on my first antidepressant medication until I was twenty-five. I had been fighting depression by exercising and going to college and just staying out of trouble. But these positive activities couldn't hold back the continual depression I was experiencing. Because I kept having difficulty handling the stresses of a full-time job, I'd get fired or eventually quit. Losing jobs only made my depression even more severe. I cried a lot and slept too much, or ate too much because eating was the only joy I felt I had left in life.

Luckily, I was seeing my first therapist at that time. She suggested that I call my general-practitioner doctor and ask to be put on an antidepressant. He gave me desipramine [brand names: Norpramin, Pertofrane; tricyclic antidepressant]. It definitely lifted my depression within two months, and I was all around happier. But it also caused me severe constipation. The other problem with desipramine was that when I rose suddenly from lying down, my blood pressure would drop fast and cause me a few moments of dizziness. Plus I had been taught by my mom that it's a shameful thing to need medicine—even of *any* kind but especially psychiatric drugs.

So after thirteen months, I went off of desipramine. That was a big mistake. My depression slowly but surely returned, and this time it was even worse because I was still getting fired from jobs. My employers tried to tell me that I'd either shut down and work slower and slower or I'd get angry and feel like I was getting abused again, so I'd start yelling at someone and then get fired.

I became suicidal again at this time, and now I was almost thirty-two. Then some more big stresses happened to me close together. I had a huge nervous breakdown and I mercifully landed in a psychiatric hospital and was promptly put on psychiatric disability. This then was the first time, at age thirty-two, that I was able to "afford" a bona fide psychiatrist, instead of a kind but not competent (in the psychiatric realm of medicine) family doctor.

When I was in the psych ward, the doctors there all told me I have post–traumatic stress disorder from all the years of severe childhood abuse. One of the recent major stresses had also been that I was informed that I definitely needed a partial hysterectomy to remove huge fibroid tumors and fix other female troubles. The ultrasound showed that my ovaries were very healthy, so I don't think any of my depressions were hormonally induced. Also when I was in the psychiatric hospital, the doctors ordered several blood tests and they all came back negative in regards to hormonal problems or any other problems. However, it did depress me off and on for four years after my operation that I couldn't have any of my own children. However, I now realize that it's for the better that I don't have any children, because with the history of abuse done to me, even with lots of financial and emotional support, I doubt I could be stable and nurturing enough to be a good parent, to even one child.

Then I was put on another antidepressant named imipramine [brand names: Tofranil, Janimine; tricyclic antidepressant]. This also gave me constipation. The imipramine did lift my depression as well as I thought it could, but every time I took the medicine I would break out in an uncomfortable sweat. It also made me crave sweets every day, too. This did not help my weight problem one bit. Over the years I had been so depressed that my main comfort and coping mechanism had been food. Sometimes I felt the joy of eating was the only positive and reliable thing I had to look forward to. So at five-feet-six-inches, by age thirty-six I weighed around three hundred pounds.

At just about this time I ran into my sister, who had also suffered from all the years of abuse. But this time she was relatively happy and stable. I'd never seen her depression-free before, so I asked her what antidepressant she was on. She said Prozac. I asked my psychiatrist if I could switch from imipramine to Prozac, after I would be tapered off the imipramine. She said yes. Because I have a history of being sensitive to psychiatric drugs—which in my case means a light dosage usually goes a long ways—I was put on the standard low dose of 20 mg. every morning. I had no constipation, no profuse sweating, no craving sweets, no bad side effects at all.

But in the second month of taking the Prozac, the pharmacist doling out the prescription made an error and ended up giving me the equivalent of 30 mg. of Prozac a day. I started sleeping too much—twelve or more hours a day. I didn't know what was wrong, so I told my psychiatrist. She wanted to look at the pills. Then she figured out the pharmacist's mistake. Now for the past ten months I've been on the correct 20 mg. dose, and I sleep the right amount and I feel happier than I've ever felt before in my entire life.

This Prozac works a lot better for me than did the desipramine and imipramine. Since my nervous breakdown I've been on disability, but within three months of taking the Prozac, I got a part-time job in food services. With the medicine and good psychotherapy, and good vocational counseling also, I have been able to keep my part-time job without shutting down or blowing up. In addition to lifting my depression and helping me to keep a job, I think the Prozac lifted my depression so well that I finally got motivated to stay on a sensible low-calorie eating plan. So now I've lost sixty-two pounds, and in the coming year I plan to lose at least another sixty pounds, with the emotional support of my weight-loss group and with exercising faithfully, too.

I have hope again, which I hadn't felt since my big nervous breakdown. I'm thirty-seven and a half now and I'm starting to feel sexy and attractive again. One thing I can't figure out is why, in the first few months of taking Prozac, I seemed to lose interest in having any sexual feelings—like it was too much trouble to bother even to masturbate—but in the last two months of the twelve months I've been on Prozac, my sex drive has returned. I don't know if it's because I have been keeping the weight off and therefore I'm starting to feel desirable or if it is because Prozac at first decreased my libido and now it's back to normal. I'll need to discuss this with my doctor in our next session.

I am no longer ashamed to be on any needed medicine—especially my antidepressant, which I feel is saving me from additional years of depression and misery. I am glad I see a psychiatrist instead of just a general practitioner, because the psychiatrists have been trained much more extensively on how psychiatric drugs affect the human body. I am grateful that Prozac exists.

One day I hope to have the stamina to work full-time and to also develop a meaningful, nurturing relationship with a decent man. Before the Prozac, I was too depressed and hopeless to even conceive of the idea that I could be happy and stable enough to maintain a close couple's relationship. With the Prozac and my professional support system and my many good friends, I have a decent future ahead of me.

John Cakars, forty-five, holds a B.A. and an M.Div. and lives in California.

My first acquaintance with Prozac was in November 1989. I had injured my back earlier that year and went to St. Mary's Hospital Spine Center. During the course of therapy I developed other physical symptoms and was referred from doctor to doctor. The neurologist said that I sounded angry and needed to see a psychiatrist. After my second session with the psychiatrist, she gave me a trial-size package of Prozac. I was to take it every day for fourteen days. I never took it for fourteen straight days, because I was not used to taking medication in the morning. I did finish the sample and was given a prescription for a hundred more. However, I lost the prescription before I could get it filled. Then I stopped seeing the doctor because my wife was against it.

I was severely depressed and my whole life was going down the tubes. I saw a clinical psychologist for twenty-six sessions in 1991 to help me deal with an assault. I stopped the sessions because my insurance only paid for twenty-six. My wife insisted that we go for joint counseling, and in January 1992 the both of us started marital therapy. During the course of therapy, I decided that I did not want to be married anymore. I felt that I had to get out to keep my mind or someone would be dead.

I consulted with an attorney, who advised me that I needed to notify the therapist of my decision. So on my birthday, April

21, 1992, I stated my intention to seek a divorce. This surprised my wife. At the next session, we told our son about what I wanted. After that, I saw the therapist by myself.

During the course of visits in May, I felt I was going out of control, so I asked about a referral for medication. I was referred to a psychiatrist, who wanted to put me on Prozac, but I was reluctant because of its reputation. I read a book about Prozac that seemed to answer most of my questions. When I went back, I stated that it would be okay. I got a prescription for Prozac and Xanax [generic name: alprazolam; antianxiety drug].

When I started taking Prozac, I got side effects of headaches, constipation, and I don't remember what else. After two weeks on the drug, the doctor asked how I was doing and gave me an extended prescription. After about three or four weeks, I noticed that I did not need to take as much Prilosec [generic name: omeprazole; antiulcer drug] as I used to. For some reason, the Prozac was reducing my reflux symptoms. When I reported that to my gastroenterologist, he preferred that I take the Prozac instead of the antiulcer medication. I noticed that while on Prozac I would start to feel more hostile and violent. These feelings were expressed one weekend, when I almost had three car accidents within an hour's time. The next day I got into an argument with one of my neighbors in the laundry room.

The next day I went to work and arranged with my therapist to be admitted to First Hospital Vallejo. I spent a week there. After I got out, instead of working through lunch, I took walks around San Francisco. I was hoping that this would relax me and help me to lose weight. What I discovered was that if people asked me for money, I would say no. If they asked again, I would say no and start to get really agitated. If they had asked me a third time, I would have considered getting violent.

The medication did nothing for my depression. All it did was to relieve my reflux and heartburn symptoms. At work, things were not getting any better but getting worse, to the point that in October 1992 I decided that I needed to be hospitalized again.

It was suggested at work that I apply for disability retirement. I asked my doctor to write a qualifying report. Since I was unhappy with her and First Hospital, I asked to be admitted to Langley Porter Psychiatric Hospital. She said okay, but by the time my admission happened, I was losing it.

The Thursday before I was to be admitted, my manager told me to give her all my work and to leave and not show up Friday either. My admission was scheduled for Monday. On Friday Langley Porter notified me that they did not have the authorization from Blue Cross for me to be admitted. I called Blue Cross and they said my original doctor was causing the problem. I called the doctor, who stated that she gave Blue Cross everything that they needed. I called back to Blue Cross and I was unable to speak to the agent handling my case but relayed the information I had. I asked if I had to commit suicide in order to be admitted. The woman on the phone said that if it was that bad, they would okay the admission from the ER. I spent the weekend in limbo not knowing what was going to happen on Monday.

Monday, around 10:00 A.M., I received a call from Langley Porter stating it was all right to come in. I also received a call from Blue Cross with the same information. I took a bus to the hospital. I had taken various medications along, with the idea of taking them before I was admitted. I was losing it.

At Langley Porter, I was taken off Prozac and Xanax and put on Klonopin [generic name: clonazepam; antianxiety drug] and Wellbutrin [generic name: bupropion; unicyclic antidepressant]. When the Wellbutrin started to take effect, it drove me up the wall. I broke out in a rash, with severe itching. After twenty-eight days of hospitalization, I was released. I had received a cortisone cream to use in the hospital, but none when I was released. The itching drove me so crazy that I was ready to peel off my skin. After another week or so the itching was not that bad. I had trouble sleeping. I wouldn't go to bed until 2:00 or 3:00 A.M. and then get up at 8:00 or 9:00 A.M. Or I wouldn't get up at all. I started to sleep in my clothes instead of changing into pjs. My depression was somewhat better, but I was still quite suicidal.

When the Wellbutrin ran out, I started taking leftover Prozac, because the antidepressants were good at relieving my stomach symptoms but not my depression. After the Prozac ran out, I convinced my gastroenterologist to prescribe it for me. He had no problem, since he preferred me to take that over the antiulcer drug.

I went back to work, but I was not allowed to resume my old position. In July 1993 I was notified that I qualified for Social Security Disability. After two months back, I was notified that the district director recommended that I should be fired. I arranged to submit a civil service disability retirement application. My first official day of civil service disability retirement was Halloween 1993.

Last year I started dating again and noticed the sexual side effects of Prozac. I had impaired erection—getting and keeping—and delayed-orgasm difficulties. I have these same problems with Zoloft.

In March 1994 I asked my G.I. doctor for something different than Prozac. The reason was that I was feeling extremely violent and angry. So I got a prescription for Zoloft. This drug has not had any effect on my feelings of anger and violence. I carry a knife at all times. Actually, all of the drugs did nothing for my depression but helped my stomach.

Jennifer Olsen, now a disabled veteran, was a specialist (SPC-E4) in the army. She is pursuing a master's in communications and loves the arts, particularly modern dance.

I first brought up the subject of antidepressant drugs with a marriage counselor when I was still trying to work things out with my husband. She said that I might benefit from them. At the time I was pregnant, so obviously drugs were out then. When my husband began following me, calling me, sending me letters, threatening to again beat me, kill me, make me miscarry, I sought a restraining order and a divorce, but my husband kept dodging the papers.

One night on the way home from the job that I despise, I was rear-ended. Of course, being pregnant, I couldn't take anything for my injuries. I felt awful. I started spotting a couple of days after the accident. Everything seemed too much to handle, so I called a doctor and arranged an abortion. I told everyone that I miscarried.

A day after the abortion, my aunt died. I remember thinking that there was no way in hell that I could face anyone in the family yet, much less attend a funeral and act normal. I was ready to scream because the pressure seemed to be too much. I called my family doctor to tell him I needed something for depression. He was out of town, so I spoke to his associate, who said he wouldn't give me anything. I was enraged that I finally had the courage to ask someone for help and he was refusing me. I screamed at him and cussed him out over the phone. He told me calmly that perhaps I should go to the emergency room.

It was then that I crossed that mental line, thinking that perhaps I was about to go to the zoo. I didn't go to the emergency room. I went to the funeral, and when I got home, I went to a counselor who was covered by my insurance, who in turn sent me to a psychiatrist.

I had never met her before that first visit, and I took an immediate dislike to her. Except for an enormous bosom, she looked like a man with makeup and a wig. She wasn't the kind of person I could talk to. I found myself in her office, staring at a very Freudian-looking set of couches while she scribbled notes about me in a manila file folder. What she could possibly be taking all those notes about, I couldn't fathom, because I had answered her few questions very haltingly.

I didn't feel like giving her much to work with; let her drag it out of me. She didn't bother. After about fifteen minutes of scribbling, she pushed a prescription for Prozac at me and told me I wouldn't feel the full effects for about two weeks.

I looked at her incredulously and let loose a deluge of questions about taking a drug that would directly affect the chemicals my brain produced. She continued to scribble in her folder, then glanced up, gave me a fake smile, and told me I would be exactly like myself before I was depressed. Immediately my stomach tightened. Who would that person be? After all, isn't this depression part of me? Isn't it why I am who I am?

So I filled the prescription. My early Prozac days were filled with a sort of philosophical self-actualizing that made me think I had finally figured out why I'm depressed: everything that I was raised to believe that life is, and should be, is full of shit. That's right, imagine waking up one day and realizing you tried everything that you were ever taught would make your life meaningful and bring you joy and happiness, and the truth was that it just wasn't going to happen, none of it.

My hippie-generation parents led me to believe that if you worked hard, kept your nose clean, and did what you were supposed to, things would work out for you. It's bullshit. I'm twenty-five years old and I have been trying to build my whole life on this stuff, and have been depressed because I bought it all. I believed it with all my heart and measured what my life was against what I thought it should be. But those dreams floated off in a late-sixties pot cloud.

It's a Generation X thing—our parents don't understand the world we grew up in. They don't realize the effects of coming of age in the age of AIDS, crack, gangs, and the recession. They don't understand the frustration and the anger of doing all the right things and still not getting the end results that are supposed to happen.

I woke up one morning so angry that I had to get up for work. I had been sleeping so well. Then I was further pissed off that I could not put on normal clothes; I had to put on business clothes. And hose and makeup and all that fucking crap. So before I even left the house I was really fucking angry. Everyone at work gave me that "Good morning" jazz and I said, "Watch out, I feel really mean."

All day I had to wait on morons and act polite, when I really wanted to tell them what I thought of them. Mine is the kind of job where you have to kiss the customer's ass, no matter how inane or stupid the customer.

The next day I called in sick. I figured I would go give the VA hospital a piece of my mind, since they didn't seem to want to help fix my body. I was almost out of Prozac and was totally out of money.

I marched right up to the psych ward. "I need to see a doctor, now," I said to a nurse. She asked me if I had an appointment.

"Nope!" I said, smiling sweetly, and sat down in a chair.

She asked, "Is this an emergency?" I started laughing, because I found that question sincerely funny. The nurse didn't think so, but got the picture. I was having my vitals taken two minutes later and talking to a screening nurse.

The doctor I got to see was pretty decent. I think I scared him, though. People in general are not accustomed to seeing women so outwardly angry. I mean, most of my girlfriends take out all their anger on themselves through anorexia, bulimia, suicide. Not me—if I ever lose it, I will take it out on everyone else.

So I spilled and spewed most everything to this doctor. At the end, he said I was not crazy, I was normal. I was very angry, very depressed, and I had every right to be. The most pressing issue was my dealing with my physical handicap. It is a certified military service–connected disability, so the doctor said I should get my Prozac free, and come to the VA for counseling. He thought I should give Prozac more time. He was worried, though.

"Do you think you need to stay in a safe place? You don't think you'll kill yourself, do you?"

I told him I would more likely be homicidal than suicidal.

He looked perturbed. "What do you feel like doing right now?"

I enjoyed being asked that question. "I would like to scream and tear all these pictures from the wall and rip them to shreds; throw the furniture around the room and destroy it and set the carpet on fire. If I were pissed off at you, I'd want to kick your teeth in. Is that normal?"

He didn't answer. He smiled and said, "Just don't do it."

When it worked, I guess, the Prozac was gradual. It sort of snuck up on me. Several of my friends and co-workers noticed a change for the better in my appearance. My friends noticed that I gradually stopped withdrawing and wanted to go out more. That funky psychiatrist was correct on one thing—I was a pretty bizarre individual before depression and am still a bizarre individual now.

The Prozac did not have the effect on me that I expected it to have. I thought that I would be some glassy-eyed, bland individual who was suddenly happy with my job, my life as it is now, and for no apparent reason, that I would start watching TV (which I hate). I thought it would even me out and make me more like everyone else, but that just isn't true.

I still feel depressed overall. The difference is that I have my good times and bad times now. Since I've been taking Prozac, if I have a bad day or a bad mood, I can realize now that maybe yesterday I was in a good mood, had a good day, or did something that pleased and satisfied me. I realize that Prozac has not changed the real me, or my bad situations, but that I am able to handle them a little more effectively.

I now have both the desire to be creative, which I've always had, and the drive and concentration to complete things, which I didn't have before Prozac. I have had more energy to exercise, so I have not only lost a little weight but have gotten firmer. This helps lift my spirits.

And as far as sex is concerned, I finally did get laid, and I am just as horny as I have always been. I sleep better now too, and my mood in the mornings has improved slightly. There were several strange stages I went through while adjusting to the drug, but eventually it all leveled out. I am still handicapped, still pissed off, still depressed, and still me. And I want to stay on Prozac because, obviously, I still have a long way to go.

Sue Beasley lives in Massachusetts.

I first heard about Prozac in 1987 when it was featured in an article in *Woman's World* magazine. The article stated this new happy pill was being tested for weight loss. At the time, I was seeing a diet doctor for my weight problem and was being prescribed a diuretic, as well as medication to decrease appetite and to increase metabolism.

I had a difficult time losing much (if any) weight while being on a twelve-hundred-calorie-a-day diet. I would've loved to try Prozac to see if it could help me shed some fat while still feeling "happy." Back then, the only way to get it was for depression and I didn't feel like I had a problem with depression to warrant seeing a psychiatrist.

Eventually my diet doctor retired. I looked over my HMO list and made an appointment with an endocrinologist, explaining that I had been seeing a diet doctor till his retirement and would like to continue getting something that might help me lose weight. I also told the doctor that I didn't have my usual high energy and was feeling a little sluggish. (I had started a job as an overnight residential counselor working in a group home for the severely mentally ill.) The doctor told me he would prescribe Prozac to help me with all my problems. Boy, was I happy. I was very anxious to see what this drug would be able to do for me: someone who is happy-go-lucky, full of energy, but dangerously overweight at 230 pounds.

Although you're not supposed to feel the full effects until after four weeks, I began feeling relaxed a week later. Things that may have made me anxious or stressed no longer seemed to bother me. I felt so much more at ease with myself. However, I was still waiting to see if it would help me lose weight. I must have been on it for six months before any of my fat started "melting away," but once it did, it happened without a great deal of effort. Sure, I was trying to keep myself busy, trying to watch what I ate. I enjoyed riding my exercise bike daily, feeling relaxed with even more energy; all the while the pounds were melting away.

I think the Prozac also helped me on the job, because I did have a stressing job that suddenly I found to be not so stressing. I definitely had more energy and was able to lose fifty pounds without a lot of effort. I was also sleeping better after being on Prozac for a while. Working the graveyard shift, I sometimes had tried to get away with not sleeping so much during the week but trying to make up for it on the weekend. With the Prozac, I allowed myself to sleep for longer periods, feeling better for having done so.

I had a steady boyfriend of eleven years who I was living with, someone who I had been content with. After being on Prozac for a few months, suddenly I wasn't so content anymore with my virtually sexless relationship with Joe. I began having an affair with Paul, who enjoyed sex. I feel that the Prozac enabled me to have an affair by not caring about Joe's feelings and only wanting to fulfill my own needs. You would have thought that I would have been nervous about having an affair right before Joe's eyes (after all, we were living together), but it seemed the Prozac made me a little more wild, and uncaring, unfeeling, of Joe.

I ended up losing 50 pounds altogether in about six months, but once I got to the 185-pound mark, it stopped. I increased my dosage to 40 mg. a day to see if that would help me start losing again. I continued to take 40 mg. a day for the next year and a half but instead of losing more weight, I gained back all that I had lost. I also started having bouts of severe depression, feeling much more depressed than I ever had in my life. I also thought of suicide.

I had read this was a possible side effect, so I stopped taking the Prozac for a few months but decided to go back on it, in another effort to lose weight. I started feeling depressed again after a while and wasn't losing weight so, again, I went off it. One time when I wanted to stop, I told my doctor and he suggested that I cut the dosage to 20 mg. instead of stopping cold; but I had already begun to stop cold.

I've just started taking Prozac again about two months ago. So far, I feel good. I am sleeping well and have cut down on snacking. I don't feel depressed but am worried that I may begin to feel depressed after I'm on it a while. It seems I don't start feeling depressed till I've been on it for at least six months. It might have been because I was taking 40 mg. a day. I am only taking 20 mg. a day now, and don't think I'll ever increase my dosage to 40 mg. again. If I do start to feel depressed with thoughts of suicide, I will most definitely stop taking it, and will probably never start again.

There is one last side effect that I almost forgot to mention. When I stopped taking Prozac the last time, I developed a dry rash on my arms and legs. It may have nothing to do with the Prozac. I still have the rash—extremely dry skin—although I'm back on the Prozac.

I stopped having an affair with Paul because he beat me up, twice. I have been celibate for a year, and faithful to Joe. I am in no hurry to have another affair no matter how sexless my life may be. Prozac did make me a little wild and crazy once, so who knows if it will happen again? Prozac is also said to be used as a painkiller, but as someone who has her share of migraines, it hasn't helped me. I don't think the migraines are due to Prozac because I've had them for many years. I do get more now, but I think that is because Paul beat my head in.

I had no problem stopping the Prozac, the few times I did. Joe could probably tell you that I am less of a bitch when I'm on Prozac. Sometimes, before, I could lose my cool and really yell at him, but I seldom do anymore. Feeling more relaxed and less anxious has certainly been something I've enjoyed about Prozac.

I have stopped and started taking Prozac three times in a four-year period. Originally, I started taking it for the weight-loss benefits, but I also enjoy the relaxed, stress-free person it makes me be. The only thing I don't like is when I start to feel very depressed or have thoughts of suicide. I know these are caused by Prozac because I didn't have these feelings before I started taking it or after I stopped. If I could lose that fifty pounds again, it would be worth it.

Meredith Guthrie lives in California.

My problems began when I was around age fourteen. I started having problems with moderate depression and had vague thoughts of suicide. By the time I was seventeen, I had panic attacks with the depression. At the time I had no idea what they were; I just thought I was dying and nobody would pay attention or take it seriously.

The panic attacks, along with paranoia, intolerance of being alone, and hallucinations that I knew were not real, persisted for about a year. I received no treatment of any kind during this period. Most of the symptoms, except for a level of anxiety, subsided for about one and a half years.

I met my future husband, and I think that temporarily distracted me for a while. The panic attacks made themselves known even more strongly than before about six months after I was married. Along with them came a severe depression. I felt lonely even with others, hopeless, sad, irritable, and didn't want to go on living. My mother brought me to a medical clinic, which referred me to a psychologist.

I saw the psychologist for a short time in therapy alone. I was then sent to a doctor who prescribed imipramine [brand names: Tofranil, Janimine; tricyclic antidepressant] and Valium [generic name: diazepam; antianxiety drug]. The doctor seemed to think that the imipramine helped me, but I never felt that it did anything except turn me into a zombie. It made me constipated, bloated, gain weight, gave me a very dry mouth, and made my ears constantly ring. It also made my blood pressure very low, which meant I was always weak and dizzy.

The Valium helped when I was severely anxious and agoraphobic, but in the long run it proved to be too depressing for me to take. I was switched to Xanax [generic name: alprazolam; antianxiety drug], which worked at least as well and had fewer side effects.

I stayed on the imipramine for about two years, even though I didn't really think it did much for me. I guess I felt I had to try something. I hated those little green pills. Because of the powerful side effects, I was always aware that I was on medication.

I changed therapists after two years, because we just didn't work together very well. I started seeing another psychologist and was taken off the imipramine and eventually off the Xanax. I felt just as good off of them as on them. I continued to have occasional bouts of panic, but nothing I couldn't tolerate on my own.

After a year or so, I started having more panic and started taking Xanax again. This worked for a while, but then I became much more depressed again. I finally convinced my therapist that therapy alone was not enough, and was given a prescription for Prozac. Because of my experience with the imipramine, my hopes of feeling better weren't very high, but I had to try something. I had also heard all the bad press stories about Prozac, which scared me a little.

My fears were laid to rest when I quickly began to feel less depressed, less anxious, and actually started enjoying some things again. I don't know how Prozac works against depression, but it does and I'm very glad it exists. After a while I was able to stop taking the Xanax, which proved to be difficult because of its addictiveness. I discovered that as long as I had some Xanax in the medicine cabinet I felt okay, but as soon as it was used up (going to the dentist, flying, or other events that were too stress-provoking to go through), I began to panic about everything.

I was taken off of the Prozac about one and a half years later. I did fine for a while, until I had to switch therapists again. I became very depressed and anxious again. Again, I started taking Prozac and Xanax. Like before, the Prozac worked wonders and I had the same love-hate relationship with the Xanax.

I did so well with my new therapist that after a year I wanted to get off the medications altogether. I stopped the Xanax and then the Prozac. I did very well for quite a while. One year earlier, I had severely injured my back and was unable to work. The disability continued for another six months, and the stress of it began to get overwhelming. I was sent to a different psychiatrist this time, who gave me Prozac and BuSpar [generic name: buspirone; antianxiety drug] instead of Xanax. This combination works much better because I notice no side effects at all, except for difficulty sleeping the first night after starting Prozac.

Despite the tremendous stress I am under because of an infuriating workers' compensation system and because I am still disabled, I am doing quite well—at least as well as somebody in my situation could be expected to do. I still have some anxiety and mild depression at times, but it is due to my situation. Once I'm out of the legal battle and, hopefully, will have at least a seminormal back, I'll be able to focus on my problems in therapy again. I'm sure that at that time I will get off all medications once and for all.

I believe Prozac is a fantastic medication. It, along with therapy, has changed my life from one of sadness and hopelessness to one of contentedness, hope, and more confidence.

I've discovered that most of my problems stem from probable repressed memories and somewhat from screwed-up relationships with my parents. Without the support of the Prozac, I would be too overwhelmed by depression and anxiety to be able to focus on these issues.

Brian Bosch is an amateur actor from New Jersey.

In my youth I was quite intelligent, to say the least. I breezed through grammar school as if I had the knowledge already programmed in my head. I graduated second in my eighth-grade class. I won awards for poetry and other creative endeavors. I am an only child. I guess I was in my own little world.

The problems began in eighth grade. I was thirteen at the time. I began to become severely depressed, as if the world was closing in on me. I also became paranoid and acquired a facial tic. This was the wonderful world known as bipolar disorder.

As if this was not enough, I also had obsessive-compulsive disorder (OCD). This menace destroyed my concentration and my life. I was constantly checking my wallet to make sure it was in my pocket. Idiotic thoughts raced around my mind in a repetitive loop. To make matters worse, I went through a stage of homosexual thinking. I am a psychology major, so I learned that this was quite normal for an adolescent to feel this way. When I saw a man on the street, I felt as if he were touching me. I did my facial tic to soothe this thought. This worked only for a second until I had to repeat the process all over. I had severe suicidal thoughts. This OCD was killing me.

In high school I got a B average, but I felt I could do better. I went to a Catholic high school that was very cliquey. I was not accepted too well and, since I lacked social skills, I kept to myself. I had my first visit to the nuthouse while in senior year. I kept all my anger bottled up until I went quite psychotic.

After high school things got a little better. I got a job selling cars and made good money. This is when my life changed forever. I met a very sexually active girl and contracted herpes. This destroyed me. I lost my job and drank like a fish. I had horrible rashes all over my body. I thought I had AIDS.

The OCD naturally compounded the problem. I obsessed all day about my pitiful condition. I attempted suicide to escape the pain. I went to my mother's psychiatrist to seek help. (Manic-depression runs in the family.) She put me on Anafranil [generic name: clomipramine; tricyclic antidepressant]. The side effects were horrendous. I became dizzy and was unable to reach orgasm. I went off that stuff and she put me on lithium [brand names: Eskalith, Lithane; mood stabilizer] and Prozac.

However, when I've stopped the lithium, Prozac sends me flying into overdrive. The manic phase doesn't always last long, but then I crash into the depressive end of the cycle. So I've learned that I need both medications.

My world is gradually getting better. I'm going to college and I've learned about OCD. I soon achieved my creativity back like when I was a kid. I feel brand-new. I can think great and the OCD is practically gone. My future looks bright and it is good to be alive again.

Lois lives with her family in California.

My husband's physician put both me and him on Prozac in January of this year. The doctor is not my primary-care physician but he knows me well, because he and I have been intensively involved in my husband's health care for the last six years.

My husband has AIDS. We had known for years that he was infected, but he was relatively well until last October, at which point he had a major all-systems crash that required nearly two months' hospitalization.

We were both so overwhelmed after my husband got sick that each of us had a kind of paralysis about everyday life. We had kept the fact of my husband's infection concealed from everyone, including our five kids, because of our fears—later justified, alas—of employment and insurance discrimination. So, when my husband became ill, we had to deal not only with his sudden life-threatening illness but also with telling our kids and closest friends, and dealing with their responses to our situation.

My husband was terminated from his job after he was in the hospital for four weeks. Suddenly we were left without his income and with a mountain of consumer debt that he had generated in a grasshopper-like spending spree, which I'm sure was an aspect of his denial of the seriousness of his illness.

Our medical insurance was and is woefully inadequate to the task of paying for his care, and besides, the insurance company is making its best efforts to kick us off the plan, because its expenditures were so very high. So the bottom line is that our bottom line is horrible, and the contemplation of that, together with my husband's looming mortality, was almost more than we could bear.

I am fifty, uninfected—that's very important—overweight, and from a Scandinavian background that seems to have depression as a hereditary trait. I am also an alcoholic's oldest daughter and spent most of my childhood gravely playing the caretaker role for my younger siblings. I guess I was a girl who just didn't know how to have fun.

When I was thirty-seven, I embarked on four years of classical Freudian analysis, which was largely unsuccessful because my therapist was inexperienced and young and I was sufficiently verbally skilled to talk rings around him, keeping the therapeutic process at bay. Other than that, the only time I have seen a therapist was for a few visits several years ago with my husband, when we were trying to resolve a conflict over when we would tell the kids their dad had AIDS.

In my real life, I am a reporter. The work is stressful because the dragon of deadlines is constantly breathing fire on my back, and because the writing I must do is very technically oriented. I am modestly compensated, so my being the sole support of the family now scares me to death.

Four years ago, our oldest child was killed in an accident. At that time, I could not take time or space to grieve but had to return to work and hit the ground running, as the cliché has it. I work in an environment where I am the oldest reporter by almost an entire generation, so none of my colleagues have had similar life experiences, in terms of marriage, family, the loss of a child, and a spouse's terminal illness, especially from a disease that bears such a social stigma. So I end up feeling very isolated much of the time.

We started with 10 mg. of Prozac, upping the dose to 20 mg., and now are taking 30 mg. daily. The first week or two I took it, I noticed nothing unusual other than a degree of edginess and a little trouble getting to sleep at night. This did not alarm me, as I am menopausal and up to then had had a great deal of difficulty sleeping, either from menopause or depression.

However, one night I found myself awake all night long. No matter what I did, I could not get to sleep. And I actually could feel something happening inside my head. There was a jittery, electrical feeling inside my skull. And I found my conscious brain rapidly shifting from topic to topic, from image to image, somewhat like the action of rapidly scanning through a computer file. I couldn't get things to quiet down inside my head, and it scared me.

This has only happened once, but I am sure that if it recurs, I will be scared again. I felt out of control, and that is not a feeling I like to have.

Even now as I write this, I notice that I am bouncing both my knees. I have always had trouble sitting still at my desk—even from the time I was a little kid—but I think I have more of a jittery body tic than I used to, and I suspect Prozac is its source.

Several times in the first month of taking Prozac, I had a funny feeling in the middle of my chest, as if a whale were turning over inside. I asked the doc if Prozac is associated with cardiac arrhythmia, and he said no. But he did begin monitoring my blood pressure and listening to my heart every time I bring my husband in for a checkup.

The big question is, am I better than I was before I started Prozac? I don't know. There are still too many things undone, tasks uncompleted, responsibilities neglected for me to call myself mentally healthy. But, given the current levels of external stress in my life, I wonder how much worse I would be if I weren't on what my husband and I call vitamin P.

I am not filled with joy all day long. I don't suddenly hear birds singing or notice flowers along the way. But, on the other hand, since beginning Prozac, I have embarked on a number of projects and tasks that have given me great pleasure, and that I had previously been unable even to consider. I made my youngest's prom dress and am just finishing my second pieced quilt. Last week I baked and decorated a wedding cake for two hundred people.

But my novel—on which I had worked consistently until my husband got sick—is languishing here in my computer. My garden, which once was the greatest pleasure of my everyday life, is now largely neglected, perhaps because its seasonal changes underscore the rapid passing of the limited number of days I know my husband has left to live with us.

The one really positive thing I can say is that, with Prozac, I have orgasms that knock my socks off. Always before, sex has been hard for me. No matter how hard I tried, orgasm was something I had to search for and concentrate on in order to make it happen. And when it did, it was all very nice, but hardly something to write home about. Well, that's not the way it is now. The orgasms are huge, and they go on forever, and afterward, I am so filled with a sense of well-being that I feel like I am floating down a warm and wonderful river. My husband jokingly calls these times my Prozac Moments.

I am afraid that, as a result of Prozac use, I have lost some of my immediate short-term memory functions, which can be very difficult if not dangerous for someone in my profession. When I am doing an interview or am at a press conference, often the most recent phrase out of a speaker's mouth will disappear out of my memory even before I can jot it down. This is worrisome because no one wants to misquote sources. The sensation I have when this occurs is that I am chasing a train of words, and the train disappears around the bend before I can catch a really good look at the caboose. Sometimes I can recapture the memory after a few minutes' reflection, but at other times, it's gone forever. I haven't really consulted to any great degree with the doc about these concerns.

I will probably continue taking Prozac indefinitely—or at least for as long as I can get the insurance to pay for it. One time I said to my husband, after we had had a particularly great Prozac Moment, that the only way they would ever get me off the drug would be to pry it out of my cold, dead hand.

John Thomas is in his forties and has two children and one cat. He lives in upstate New York.

Nine years ago I was hospitalized for drug and alcohol addiction. Before I was admitted, I made a serious suicide attempt. After treatment I felt better but continued to feel depressed and thought constantly of suicide. I must have written two suicide notes a day to my exasperated wife. I returned to work and found that I got some measure of relief focusing on other people's problems. I am a physician.

After several months the depression became more cyclic in nature. Interspersed were what only later were diagnosed as manic episodes. There are three different women in the area with new cars I bought for them—typical manic behavior. I left my wife and family and took up a series of relationships.

Three years after my hospitalization I became painfully, suicidally depressed. Suicide became a fixed option. After all, my own father had killed himself only the year before. Finally I tried an overdose of drugs. I was found the next day, unconscious. Finally I awoke. How embarrassing. I was a physician with expert pharmacological knowledge and access to deadly drugs. I had failed at suicide. It is much more difficult to kill someone than I realized.

During the subsequent psychiatric hospitalization, I acquired my first psychiatrist. He recommended that I take desipramine [brand names: Norpramin, Pertofrane; tricyclic antidepressant].

As a recovering alcoholic, I did not want to take any mind-altering drugs. After much convincing, I agreed to desipramine therapy.

I was on desipramine for six years. It did not remain consistently effective. I became overworked, exhausted, and depressed. I made another suicide attempt. Another hospitalization followed. Eventually I was discharged, still on desipramine. One particularly bothersome side effect, chronic mild urinary retention and hesitancy—an old man's problem—had a definite effect on my self-esteem. I was put on Prozac with the desipramine. It jazzed me up terribly, precipitating a manic episode, in which I lost a job. I didn't wait to be fired but quit on my own, with expletives.

Last January I decided to stop the desipramine on my own. A physician who treats himself has a fool for a doctor. Not long after, I became depressed, of course. I decided to try Prozac again, this time alone.

Prozac did not transform my personality. It made me hyperirritable. It also caused delayed ejaculation, delayed to the point of infinity. My current girlfriend was very sexually demanding and this was not a tolerable state of affairs. The three-year relationship was terminated.

I ended up in a motel with a gun. This time I asked for help. A friend came and got me into another psychiatric hospital. This was my fourth, with each hospitalization occurring every three years. My history was reviewed in much greater depth than ever before. A diagnosis of bipolar affective disorder—manic-depressive illness—was made; lithium was prescribed in addition to desipramine.

I am not entirely stabilized, but I am optimistic that in a few months I will be able to return to work. When I return, I will be more sensitive to the diagnosis of depression, particularly bipolar depression.

Lillian Hooks lives in Georgia.

I was bulimic, depressed, and without hope for a healthy life. I knew that I was in danger of myself, suicidal, destructive, and constantly melancholic. I didn't have any real friends. I would occasionally meet people, but they sensed my desperation and loneliness, and I was too impatient to allow a friendship to grow. I would smother and kill the opportunity.

My parents divorced when I was three. My mother, who remarried shortly after the divorce, moved my older brother and me around until she found the place that made her happy. Freshly fourteen, I moved out of my mother's house and into my father's. I lived with my unmarried father and brother for four years. During my sophomore year of high school, I became bulimic. I made outstanding grades, headed many clubs, and was a sturdy athlete. I was pretty and popular, yet I hated myself.

I went to college and promptly failed out. I did not attend classes, but instead went to bars five nights a week and practiced bulimia the rest of my time. During that time, my bulimia worsened, I attempted suicide, and became temporarily pregnant.

My finances were in disarray, mostly because I spent so much money on food (about one hundred dollars per week for myself) for binging and purging, and I tried to cover up my spending from my father, who supplied my allowance. My car was always maintained until my boyfriend totaled it; then I was without a car for a year, during which I used my bike.

It was at this time that I sought psychotherapy. My doctor quickly placed me on Prozac to help with my bulimia. I instantly felt better and it curbed my impulses to abuse food. After taking Prozac, it was as though I swallowed a miracle. I felt free and unburdened. I knew my life wasn't perfect, that the real problems were not gone. It was as though my thoughts were now pinned neatly on a clothesline rather than swirling endlessly and violently in my mind.

I didn't feel high or strung-out, just steady and constant. I felt more powerful than my problems and felt that I could now tackle them, as though I now had the strength and hope to overcome them. I felt much better, which meant to me, simply sane.

I didn't experience any significant side effects other than fatigue, and that not constantly, but I did take a lot of naps.

Several months after starting Prozac, I moved to a different city, left my boyfriend, started a new school, made friends, got involved in extracurricular activities, and vowed to myself that I would start over and do it right this time. My problems, of course, didn't go away—family, lack of self-esteem, indecision about career choices—but it all didn't seem to matter so much because I wasn't bulimic anymore. I felt that I had conquered the worst and that everything else would work out eventually.

When I decided to stop taking Prozac about nine months after I began, my roommate said that she was scared of and for me. She said that I was quite moody, but I didn't notice this myself. A few months later I stopped taking Prozac.

The years following were a constant mood swing. I dated several men seriously, but nothing seemed to make me happy. I felt constantly weighed down or as if a black cloud was following above my head. I didn't like being alone, but I felt comfortable being a loner. I managed to keep up my grades in school and participate in extracurricular activities.

Last September I met my husband. I knew the moment I saw him that he was the one I needed. We embarked upon a relationship and everything was perfect. But my predictable breakdowns continued, along with night sweats that had begun several months before. Over Christmas I begged my father to let me start again with a therapist, mainly so I could get a prescription for Prozac. I knew that this was what I needed. He refused, and I felt lost and doomed to be perpetually sad.

Then I read in a popular women's magazine that birth-control pills reduce the amount of serotonin in the brain. I found out that Prozac helps replace a lack of serotonin. I continued intense research. Through studying women's books, health manuals, and vitamin books, I made the decision to cease my use of birth-control pills, having taken them for eight years. I began taking vitamin B_6, which naturally helps produce serotonin. At first I was afraid to take as many vitamins as I was, but I felt my body wanting them and I promised myself that I would wean myself off when the time was right. I felt stable once again, as if I were back on Prozac. I, without consciously thinking about it, slowly decreased my use of B_6.

As I write, I am happily married and have graduated from college. I feel better than I ever have in my life. My bulimia is totally under control—I can't remember the last time I purged. I have not taken Prozac for several years now. I occasionally take B_6 now, when I feel I need it. I still battle emotional chaos on a daily basis, but I know that I have the power to win. I understand that it will take time to mend twenty-four years of ignoring my self.

Dan Leiber, a scientist, is happily married, with two children.

In 1991, I decided, with my wife, to make a major job change and move from New Jersey to Massachusetts. I felt the need to grow professionally and thought nothing about picking up and moving by myself to Massachusetts for a few months before my family could sell our house and then follow me up north.

In late September I moved into an apartment. I slowly realized that I was feeling isolated, lonely, and very unhappy after my family left from a weekend visit in October. I remember feeling sad and a bit afraid of the dark gradually over those last few months in 1991. I may have become depressed without knowing it.

The job was not what I thought it would be, and people did not treat me well. I remember saying over and over to myself: "I moved up here alone, I don't have a family, I don't have my own office, computer, or telephone, I don't have a paycheck [I wasn't paid for two months], I don't have a faculty appointment, and I don't have any friends up here."

My family moved up to Massachusetts in January 1992. We bought a house and moved in that same month. By late January I was being ignored by my apparent colleagues at work, and by March I was fired. I had five months' severance pay.

I started jogging in April and had thirty-six letters sent out inquiring about employment in eastern Massachusetts by

Passover. Nothing much came of these letters, but I lost weight, maybe fifteen pounds. I filed for unemployment in the summer of 1992. I did have the opportunity of a consulting job, beginning in October.

In November, I visited a career counselor and said to her, "I'm having obsessive thoughts about moving back to New Jersey." She suggested some professional therapy. In late November, I had one excellent job interview, leading to a job offer in December; then my father-in-law died. The new job started in January 1993. After the first week, I started to fall apart.

I woke up most mornings about four o'clock. I would be unable to sleep and would think obsessively about how it was my fault things did not work out, how I had hurt my family, torn my children away from their friends, run away from my own friends; I wanted, even planned how, to change jobs again, even after finally getting a new one, so that we could move back to New Jersey. This happened almost every morning.

In February 1993 I saw a psychiatrist, saying I came in only for a tune-up, and totally rejected the idea of medication. I had therapy once a week, and talked about sleeping on my job, and about my fears of losing the job due to my poor performance.

In early March, I woke up one Saturday morning at five o'clock convinced I was trapped. I was so tired and so much responsible for all the bad things that had happened, I decided to lie down in the car for a while with it running and with the garage door closed and get some sleep there. I got up and walked to the door, and knew I couldn't do it.

At 7:30 A.M. I called my therapist to say I needed something more, medication, if necessary. He suggested hospitalization, if I wanted it; I said no. He said to come in with my wife in the afternoon.

That afternoon I remember being almost without hope, so very negative about myself and my life. I recall having numb cheeks and an inability to smile or make clear decisions. I had felt like that for nearly two or three months. The psychiatrist, my wife, and I talked about major depressive episodes, medications, and how they would help.

The psychiatrist said there would be a period of trials with different medications, and I might not know for six weeks or more if a medication was helping. My wife (who also has had major depressive episodes in her adult life) suggested I talk with my brother, who also had been treated for depression. The psychiatrist suggested calling my brother immediately to ask about what medications had helped him, because often the biochemical pathways that are altered in the depressed brain are similar in other family members.

That first conversation was the best I ever had with my brother. He said imipramine [brand names: Tofranil, Janimine; tricyclic antidepressant] (which my doctor was going to suggest first) was ineffective, made him hallucinate, and caused him some heart problems. He had been taking Prozac for about four months and was feeling much, much better than he had for a long time.

The psychiatrist said, "We have our answer." I felt there was hope I would finally feel better. If there is a "biology of hope" effect, I was feeling it that Saturday in March when I took my prescription to the pharmacist.

The first one or two nights on Prozac made me feel jittery as hell. If I thought I had trouble sleeping before Prozac, it seemed nearly impossible now. I was afraid to sleep because it was so disruptive and so unsatisfying.

For four or five weeks, I forced myself to move, to get out of bed, to wash myself, to go to synagogue, twice a week sometimes, to pray, to try to keep going until the medication started to work in my brain. Most important, my brother and the psychiatrist had said to call anytime. I called my brother almost daily, from home or from work. He knew exactly what I was going through. He said to make a list with one thing on it, and try to get it done. Don't expect to do more than that, lay low, and keep calling him. I did.

About six weeks later, I remember saying in therapy that I wasn't much concerned now with the medication and how I was feeling.

"Fuck it, there is too much work to do," I said.

Both the psychiatrist and I laughed. I was feeling better. All along, one of the best measures of my own level of depression was my sense of humor. My ability to laugh at things and myself was the best marker of how I was feeling. My recovery progressed first by sleeping better, having more energy, then having many fewer obsessive thoughts, and finally, by laughing more.

I stayed on the medication for about ten months. I *VERY* gradually tapered off it, perhaps more slowly than anyone in history, and found I was able to sleep, to think clearly, and to laugh without it.

In retrospect, I grew closer to my brother than I've ever been. In some sense, I rediscovered my brother and how much I needed him and his love. I discovered what my wife had gone through, and was more empathetic and more in love with her because of my depression and recovery from it. Most important for me, I know I can recover from severe depression again if I have to.

PJ Suttle lives in South Carolina.

Let me describe my Before Prozac persona. I consider myself to have been an achiever. If I set out to accomplish a task, I make it my main priority to finish successfully what I've begun. I've never had any trouble expressing myself verbally or nonverbally. At the same time, I've always been an emotional person. However, I've been a very melancholy individual. And this is what has led me into a state of sadness and depression.

With an active imagination as well as a tendency to wander off in my own world, I suffered the onslaught of melancholy or a glum mood, leading sometimes to crying fits or just the blahs. I don't have to tell you that we all get depressed now and then. It's just that I'd let this feeling overcome me and basically control my life. I would have crying fits and junk-food binges as well as pop off at my husband or the basset hounds—we're talking serious mood swings! And the worst thing was that I knew I was depressed.

I've always been a type A personality, naturally hyperkinetic. As a child, my mother regulated my intake of sugars to keep me from bouncing off every wall. As an adult, I still keep the sugars in check, even though I have been known to consume massive doses of sugar to get that instant-energy sugar jolt. You may wonder, what does this have to do with taking antidepressants? Well, it goes along hand in hand as far as I'm concerned.

I thought being an educated person, albeit with limited knowledge in psychology, I could handle this on my own. No such luck. Even my calm, supportive husband couldn't do anything to help. We're completely opposite. Opposites do attract! I stimulate John, and he brings me down a few octaves to normal. What began to happen was when I'd get upset, he'd get calm. If I was going off, he'd even get calmer! This I found very disturbing. I just wanted him to get upset with me—not calm! He suggested I speak with my doctor the next time I got my physical.

When I had my yearly physical, I inquired whether or not a pill could be an answer to my mood swings, crying fits, and melancholy. My doctor ordered every imaginable test under the sun to determine whether I was suffering from some disease. He concluded that I have a chemical imbalance. And with an antidepressant such as Prozac, I could conceivably get back to an even keel.

I believe that work-related stress led me into my depression. The counselor I chose has assured me that it's okay to be slightly neurotic; however, it could be a problem if my behavior leads to acts of violence. She suggested stress management in lieu of counseling, gave me wonderful tapes to listen to, and told me to continue to use breathing relaxation techniques. I've given up my consumption of caffeine and slowed my intake of M & M's, both of which were contributing to my jitteriness and aggressive behavior.

My doctor told me that his minimum treatment time is six months. He said that it would take at least two weeks for Prozac to get into my system. And during this period, I might suffer from night sweats, sleeplessness, double vision, feelings of being jittery, nausea, diarrhea, dry mouth, an increased libido, or anxiety. He was correct. I did experience all of the above.

The first month I began the Prozac treatments, I really suffered from insomnia.

The increased libido mentioned before, well, my sex life had been pretty much routine and stagnated. Don't get me wrong, it was great—just not frequent, but it was the quality, not the quantity. Now it's the quality and the quantity! My pharmacist warned me about this side effect. One wants sex frequently; however, achieving orgasm is another tale of woe. Luckily for me, my husband and partner, John, understands and is very industrious when it comes to pleasing me and fulfilling my needs.

John's even mentioned that there is definitely an improved difference in my personality. I am now more calm. I don't pop off at him or the dogs over nothing. Rather, now it's over something legit, if I'm disturbed or annoyed by some action.

As of this writing, I've been on Prozac five months. I plan to take the three remaining refills of the medication. Once I've reached the final refill, I will wean myself off the drug by taking it every other day for two weeks. If, after I've finished taking the medicine, my melancholy tendencies return, then I will more than likely decide to find a physician in the new area I am moving to.

I'm certain that I will always be a type A personality. However, I must continue to strive to be calm. Or at least keep the company of calm people. Hopefully, their serenity will rub off on me.

Margie Banashek lives in Florida.

I grew up in a home where drinking and fighting were daily occurrences. Deep down, I knew my parents loved me, but I always felt guilty if I tried to take any attention away from their problems. There were no safe places in my house, and all our relatives were equally unhinged.

School was even worse, as my mother was under the impression that we three ingrates (my brother, sister, and me) should get a Catholic grammar-school education. Between home and school, I experienced periods of manic outbursts, sheer terror, and depression. As I grew into my teens, my mood swings became more frequent, but no one noticed.

Throughout high school and into art school, I became progressively stranger. My father pretended not to know me if we met in public. I stayed away from home and drank with my maladjusted friends. In 1970, without consulting anyone, I married a rock musician and we communicated mostly through a haze of drugs and alcohol. In 1975, the marriage ended and I immediately stepped into a new relationship with Richard, who has remained my sole support for the past eighteen years.

Around then, my mother was diagnosed with cancer and died at age forty-nine. One year later, my father died of a cerebral hemorrhage at fifty-one. The family scattered and I took charge of the estate. I made bad decisions and sold the house, which was torn down and leveled into a parking lot. I eventually lost the job I had held for seven years. My losses were overwhelming; I became withdrawn and suicidal.

Richard, who was now my sole support, was astonished to see the changes occurring in me. I slept most of the time, and I was paralyzed in fear about talking on the phone. Once attractive, I was now twenty-five pounds overweight and hid my face under masses of overly permed hair. I completely became isolated and began to live in my head more and more. I engaged in rantings and ravings, and when I wasn't sobbing uncontrollably, I was curled up in a fetal position. I depleted any of Richard's financial gains as my illness demanded all his time and effort to keep me under control.

In 1980, after three years of insanity, Richard persuaded me to seek psychiatric help. I was diagnosed as manic-depressive and prescribed lithium [brand names: Lithane, Eskalith; mood stabilizer] and Pamelor [generic name: nortriptyline; tricyclic antidepressant]. I was relieved that God answered my prayer with the magic pill that would change my life. However, I was disappointed with the results of my pills.

Because the lithium leveled off the manic highs, my depression was more prevalent. The Pamelor did nothing but cause annoying side effects like dry mouth, constipation, hand tremors, and swollen legs. After a few months, I was taken off Pamelor and prescribed imiprimine [brand names: Tofranil, Janimine; tricyclic antidepressant], which I took for the next eight years.

I endured dry mouth and constipation; my hair showed signs of being brittle, and my skin broke out with sebaceous cysts. I had no sexual desire and I was endlessly fasting to lose weight.

Although the violence had toned down in the house, I continued to engage in fierce, all-night debates with Richard. He viewed me as the mental case who needed constant supervision.

I, on the other hand, became a born-again antidepressant evangelist. I was proud to carry the message of the depressed and told everyone I met: bus drivers, evading relatives, potential employers. I thought to tell meant I was better.

I lived like this for the next several years, experiencing ups and downs but never solving any of my real problems. I didn't have a clue that I was still depressed and deeply disturbed. I had not grown emotionally for a long time and, in 1986, began to drink again. Alcohol played havoc with the medication, and soon I was off and running. In a rage and out of control, I became vicious and dangerous to myself and the people around me. What little possessions I had gained were slowly being taken away.

Again, I crawled to my psychiatrist and demanded a cure. He took me off imiprimine and prescribed Prozac and Twelve-Step meetings. The combination of these two was the catalyst that changed my life. Within two weeks of taking Prozac, my depression was gone. The only side effect remaining was dry mouth, but that may have been caused by lithium. My thinking was suddenly crystal-clear. I was aware of everything around me. I could handle walking and chewing gum at the same time.

Prozac seemed to have trained my brain to respond undepressed; I finally knew what it felt like to not be depressed. I attended Adult Children of Alcoholics meetings and from there, went to Al-Anon and AA. I was able to share my story at meetings and received so much positive feedback it overwhelmed me. For the first time in years I had friends—friends who identified with my experience, strength, and hope. I cruised on this new high for a few years, but began to feel unfulfilled as I listened to recovering alcoholics discuss their first year of sobriety. Descriptions of putting down the drink and being on an emotional roller coaster confused me. I was dealing with only two basic feelings: complacency and anger. Emotionally, I felt dead. I reasoned that I was substituting medication for sobriety; I was dependent on it.

Suddenly, I didn't feel part of the group anymore. I felt overmedicated. After wrestling with it in my mind for a long time, I made the decision to stop taking medication. I consulted with a new psychiatrist and we both decided to have me stop cold turkey while he monitored my progress closely for several months. I felt very supported by him, Richard, and my AA group. After several months of no major setbacks, I felt positive that I had taken the right step. My dry mouth was gone; in fact, I was salivating heavily now. I joined an aerobics class and started weight lifting in case my violent rages returned. I was in shape for the first time in my life. On medication, I couldn't exert any energy, or I'd feel nauseated and lightheaded.

The best thing that occurred, though, was the kaleidoscope of emotions I was experiencing. Feelings I'd avoided since I was a child: sadness, resentment, joy, jealousy, sympathy, concern, and grief. I finally grieved the death of my parents. I understood fear, doubt, and insecurity.

It has been four and a half years since I stopped taking Prozac and lithium, but the journey to recovery continues. The most difficult lesson I've had to swallow is that life's problems still exist. I go through periods of depression still, and encounter situations I find intolerable. Sometimes I actually believe I should never feel depressed. I struggle through my days like everyone else, trying to find the answers and be happy, joyous, and free.

Prozac was like a spiritual awakening for my chemically depressed brain. Now, spiritual awakenings come in baby steps. I am aware that I choose my moods these days, and I must work hard to not fall into habits of choosing the negative. I remind myself daily that I am not my emotions.

I try very hard to live my life without medication. Sometimes I think it would be easier to just take it again, but my heart tells me no. To anyone else I would say yes, yes, yes. If you've never experienced life without the heavy veil of depression, Prozac or another antidepressant might enlighten you. You might feel peculiar once off the meds, but you will feel like a contributing peculiarity.

Molly is a biochemistry graduate student based in Colorado.

I started seeking help for my depression in the middle of my senior year of college. It seemed as though everything was going wrong or too stressful all at once. My job was crazy; my aunt died; my father was hospitalized; my mom, an alcoholic, increased the amount she drank because of my father's hospitalization; I was applying to graduate school.

The frustrating thing about this depression was how it crept up on me virtually unnoticed: one day I couldn't stop crying at a staff meeting, and my supervisor made me seek help. Once it was pointed out to me and, perhaps more important, somebody else believed I was depressed, it was easier to believe myself. I began to see the little things that indicate depression. I was on the varsity cross-country team and I'd lost interest in running. I could not keep my dorm room clean, which was unusual for me. I started taking longer to fall asleep because I needed to cry. Ordinarily my favorite time of the day was early in the morning. I liked to get up before the rest of the dorm and use the quiet to study. By February, I'd wake up twenty minutes before class to rush to get there on time, and still I'd need a nap in the afternoon.

It was a great deal more difficult to study, though my class attendance was perfect. My grades, though not poor, reflected my lack of interest. I was barely able to complete the applications to grad school, and if not for a caring adviser/mentor, I would not have completed them at all. Finally, because it was our senior year, my friends wanted to party all the time. They seemed to be on Fast Forward while I was on Pause. Trying to keep up with them absolutely exhausted me. It was easier to stay home by myself.

After seeing a therapist three times, she suggested I consider antidepressants. I absolutely refused. I felt that if I could cope with depression as a child (I had depressions at ages ten and sixteen, which I had grown out of), all by myself, I could certainly cope better as an adult. After all, if the sixteen-year-old me could contemplate suicide for several months and prevent myself from doing anything, certainly the twenty-two-year-old could.

Taking a drug would be admitting that I was weak, that not only was I not stronger than the problem but that it had defeated me. My attitude, combined with my judgment of the college counseling center's overuse of psychoactive drugs, resulted in a firm resolve to resist medication.

After graduation things remained the same—I was still depressed, still seeing a therapist, and still crying myself to sleep at night—but I found a job I really liked at a hospital. Yet I did not want to leave for graduate school. Eventually, with the encouragement of my therapist, I took a year off from school. I was disappointed, but I was in no shape to start school; it did feel as though a great weight had been lifted from my shoulders when I decided to delay.

Throughout the fall I bantered back and forth with my therapist about taking Prozac. In my free time at work, I read more about depression; it began to seem like drugs were the only step I could take next. The more I thought about it, the more I felt I had no choices left. I went to see the doctor shaking in my socks. I was terrified he would not believe that I was depressed, and if he didn't, I would have no other options. The doctor prescribed Prozac.

I was too nervous to fill the prescription right away. I worried my driving would be affected, but I started taking it before I went home because if I started to procrastinate, I'd never do it. I was determined not to tell my parents. I felt they wouldn't understand, and I couldn't explain. I almost choked at dinner when my cousin blurted conversationally, "Do you know anyone on Prozac?" She'd read an article about the amounts of people taking Prozac. I never have told her she was sitting next to someone who was taking it.

I was determined to be patient with the drug. The pessimist in me expected nothing, yet part of me expected a miracle. Not a whole lot happened. But slowly I began to realize I wasn't crying as much, and when I wanted to cry I had a little more control. There was no more crying at work. After a month or so I returned to the doctor, who increased the dosage to two pills (40 mg.) per day. I wasn't happy about this, but I figured I ought to try it.

I got the same gradual improvement as before. The one thing I did notice was my extreme sensitivity to touch. In the hospital one workday, I was jostled in the crowded cafeteria. It was a mere accidental brush. But I whipped around and, quite out of character, prepared to yell at the perpetrator of this crime. Fortunately, good sense stopped me when I realized the evil person was an elderly woman with a walker struggling to carry a tray. This sensitivity has decreased some, but not entirely, with time.

Shortly thereafter I moved across country to begin graduate school. It has been a rocky transition, as I have been very homesick for the first time. I believe the Prozac has helped with the adjustment.

For me, one of the ethical debates I have had taking this drug is about my relationship with my boyfriend. We started dating after I started the Prozac. He has known about most of my history from the outset, and he says it's all okay with him. But I wonder if we'd be going out if it weren't for Prozac. Not that I regret dating him, but what if this relationship has more to do with my taking this drug than with just me? I keep wondering if it's okay. After all, if I were under the influence of alcohol or illicit drugs, the answer would be a steadfast "No, it's not okay." But, like much of life, this question remains in a fuzzy, gray area.

On the whole, Prozac is a hard drug to describe. I still feel like me. Sometimes it's hard to remember to take it because I feel fine. On the other hand, there's abject fear of what will or could happen if I stop taking it. And, worst of all, there are no hard-and-fast answers. Nor will there ever be.

Linda Sailor is a licensed professional counselor based in the West.

I am a therapist and have been on Prozac about a year. I have not tried any other antidepressants.

I have not noticed a *HUGE* change but little changes. It seemed to work very gradually to make me not as anxious, and I don't take things as seriously as I once did.

I tend to be a very workaholic, responsible, caring person, and sometimes I care too much! I think Prozac has helped me detach a little and also focus. I think I have a little ADHD [attention deficit hyperactivity disorder] also, and it has helped that.

The only side effect I had was a little insomnia at first. I think it has also helped my PMS [premenstrual syndrome]. I am almost menopausal, too (age fifty), so I feel it may help that too, or is it the placebo effect?

Gary R. Hill is a forty-one-year-old carpenter/draftsman based in Nashville, Tennessee.

At the age of twelve I first remember feeling depressed, feeling a sense of impending doom. I began self-medicating at sixteen—there was nothing recreational about my drug use. By the time I was twenty, I was almost solely using my drug of choice: alcohol. Drinking and depression were the only reality I would know for the next twenty years. Detox and rehab became routine, as did trouble with the law.

In January 1994 I finally was able to afford health insurance and began taking Prozac, with bimonthly therapy and monthly visits to a psychiatrist for refills. Without this insurance, I would never have been able to afford Prozac and all that it entails. (The minimum dose of 20 mg. per day cost me $220 per month, or $2,640 per year. Maybe if we all said the drug doesn't really work, the price will come down.)

When I first began taking Prozac, I didn't feel anything for a week or two. Then I began to have a tingling numbness in my lips and a lot of indigestion, which lasted another week or two until the stomach upset subsided, although the tingling lips come and go. Other than that I've had no side effects—as long as I stay on the medication. Woe are they who have been on it for several months and decide one Sunday that they can make it till Friday's paycheck for a refill, as I did. I came down with severe "ants in my pants" and wore a figure eight in my rug chasing my brain around the living room, alternately pausing to howl at the moon and to check for growth of my facial hair and eyeteeth. That's when I said to myself, "I guess there really *is* something in those little pills."

Please excuse the levity, but because of Prozac I've had restored my cherished sense of humor. Last Christmas I was emotionally paralyzed, despondent. I'd cry at the drop of a hat. I was no longer thinking of suicide, I was literally building my own casket, as I am a fine craftsman. My friends and family were prepared for the worst.

Now everyone says that they're not sure who I am, but whatever I did with Gary, don't bring him back. I couldn't agree more. Before, in a grocery I would become almost violently agitated or have an anxiety attack while standing in line. Now I'll chat with the person behind me about the bearded baby on the cover of the *National Enquirer* and chuckle as the cashier (inevitably) changes her register tape.

Prozac has been a most important vehicle for the relearning of my talents, my good, and my worth. Doors are opening for me that I never recognized as being existent. My clarity of thought now allows my imagination to fly free—even to the point of being able to understand the Native American saying: "The future is just one step behind you."

I am now content, less argumentative, more patient, and more sure. (Not bad for an atheist.) As for Prozac's effect on my sexuality, well, I can't say I've noticed any change. But heck, at forty-one years old sometimes you're Tarzan and sometimes you're not.

JoAnn Kunzel lives in Washington.

I had been seeing a counselor for about a year when she suggested that I start taking an antidepressant. I had been going through some difficult times. I was continually having problems with my job, and I was also having some problems getting along and communicating with my housemate. I was always crying and depressed. I was having trouble eating and sleeping, and I felt that I was in a "mood" at work and socially. I did not have much patience at work and found myself getting angry at people very quickly. Basically, I was very unhappy.

Seeing my counselor always helped, but I was getting frustrated because I kept going to my sessions but it just seemed that nothing was clicking. I would get more frustrated and become more depressed. All along I felt like a failure that I couldn't get myself together. I often had thoughts of suicide and called the crisis line several times. It seemed that things would go well for a while and then I would start thinking too much and get depressed and fall back into a slump.

I often felt that I didn't have any friends because they were tired of listening to me cry and be unhappy. I felt very lonely and alone. A friend told me he would only be able to be a "fair-weather" friend and this made me think a lot. I started thinking that I was not the person I wanted to be. I had always been told that I was a happy and positive person, and I realized that this was no longer true.

So I agreed to try to take Prozac on a trial basis. I had to think about it for a few weeks beforehand. My mother was a chronic alcoholic and was always off and on antidepressants, and I lost a lot of respect for her because she couldn't get herself together without drugs. Also, my oldest brother has been diagnosed as a manic-depressive and is always on some kind of drug or another. I have also lost a lot of respect for him. While he is taking the drugs, he always seems out of it and he seems like a different person. I was afraid of becoming my mother and brother, which was very scary to me.

I was also always very concerned about the side effects. I talked to a very good friend of mine who is always supportive of me, no matter how many times I've called her crying uncontrollably. She told me her partner was taking an antidepressant and how it changed his life, and how taking something could maybe change mine. I was desperate and started taking the Prozac, and things started to get easier. I felt I didn't lose control as much and I was happier with myself. At that time I didn't notice any side effects. I was taking a very small dosage (a half a pill).

But I was still obsessed with a particular person in my life. J. had expressed extreme dislike toward me, saying he never wanted to have anything to do with me. This wouldn't have been so difficult but he started dating a friend of mine, and I felt our friendship changed because J. disliked me so. When I thought about J., I would get very sad and I always felt like a terrible person. No one in my thirty-four years had ever said those things to me. J. had told me that I treated him like a child and that on several occasions I was rude to him. I wanted to explain some things to him, but he never gave me the opportunity—I feel badly that he never gave me that chance. I was obsessed by the fact that J. felt so strongly about me. I felt like a failure in life to have someone reject me so. I had dreams almost every night about him, and they were always dreams where we talked and had a good time together. The dreams made me sad because I knew that they would never come true.

I shared this all with my counselor, and she suggested that I start taking Paxil, because it was supposed to be better than Prozac at treating obsessive behavior. I took it for quite a while, a few months. I started feeling better and less obsessed with J. But I started having terrible night sweats. I also noticed that I was dreaming a lot, and the dreams were always very vivid and often scary. I would wake up in the middle of the night, and my nightgown and sheets would be drenched. I couldn't figure out why I was sweating so much. Finally I went to the doctor and she said that it was a side effect of Paxil.

I went back to my counselor and she then suggested Zoloft. I took this for another few months and I was able to maintain a good outlook knowing that J. felt so negatively about me. I didn't notice any side effects for a while, and then the night sweats started again. My counselor and I decided to go back to Prozac, because I didn't notice any side effects from the Prozac.

Things in my life started to improve again. I started feeling better about myself socially and at work. I was starting to gain more confidence. I felt like I had some very good friends who were very supportive, and I started being happier. Things at work got better and I started spending my time on other things besides thinking about J. I started to feel like I needed to be more and more organized, and I cleaned and organized at home and at my workspace. This also made me feel better. I started spending more time alone, and I enjoyed it more and more. I started thinking again that I wasn't such a terrible person.

But still every once in a while something would set me off and I would cry for an entire day and have to call in sick for work, and this concerned me. These times were few and far between, so it seemed that I could handle them. Mostly these times happened because I felt like I could not communicate things accurately, and I always felt misunderstood.

While taking the Prozac, I started getting headaches every day. I thought at first that they were caused by stress and dealt with them by taking aspirin. Then I started reading about the side effects of Prozac and realized that the headaches could be caused by the Prozac. I had also noticed quite a bit of weight gain, about ten pounds, and I felt bloated. I stopped taking the Prozac without consulting my counselor, and slowly the headaches went away.

Well, I had tried three different antidepressants and they all had some sort of side effects. This made me frustrated, because I had finally started to feel better about myself and feel more hopeful and in a better mood overall.

It has been about a month since I have taken any antidepressant. I've noticed that I no longer get the headaches and I feel less bloated and my dreams seem more normal. I realize that without taking the drugs my life seems to be getting better all the time. I felt the side effects weren't worth the emotional stability. I have been trying to have a better outlook on everything, and try to remain positive about all things at home and at work. I think taking the drugs taught me that it was possible to live a much happier life, and now that I know what it is like, I hope that I can try to feel better on my own without taking the antidepressants.

Jan Fogel is a forty-two-year-old woman who lives in Washington, D.C.

I started taking Prozac when it first came on the market, in 1988. A few years before that, I'd been on some tricyclic that left me jittery, nervous, racing, and made me gain close to fifteen pounds (I'm five-feet-two-inches; about 100–105 pounds normally). It was worse than just being depressed and weepy, so I stopped.

Prozac left me with little appetite, nausea, and diarrhea for about a week; then I started feeling lighter somehow. I no longer felt the side effects, and was less deep in depression. I took one 20 mg. pill each morning.

People commented on how well I looked, that my general outlook was better, that I seemed more comfortable with myself. I also felt less anxious, less down-in-the-dumps, more willing to go out and *do* things.

After several months I cut back to one Prozac every other day. There was even a two- to three-month period where I was taking only one pill a week. The doctor expressed doubt that this could be helping, but since I was obviously doing well and feeling fine, she let me continue on one pill a week.

Continuing to feel so good, I decided to go off Prozac altogether eight to ten months later. I could tell when my system was clear of the drug; there was a dropping of mood, but so slight I didn't worry about it. In all, I was clear of all medication for four months, and only toward the end of the third month did I start feeling miserable again. I'd outline the lines on the palms of my hands in red or black ink; sometimes I'd have to leave home so I wouldn't call my therapist; I spent lots of time in bed sleeping or trying to; I also tore off layers of skin on the palm of my right hand.

So, back on Prozac on a daily basis—until 1992, when I'd do alternate days or every third day. Prozac was no longer available from the psychiatrist who had monitored me (not my therapist, who had no medical degree), and at $1.89 a pill, it was expensive. (Now, in 1994, Prozac is $2.08 a pill.) I also went off the drug during the summer and/or early fall when I always seemed to feel better. I also left therapy for five months after several months of one session monthly.

Then I began feeling worthless, lethargic, self-destructive—peeling my palm again, lining up all my knives in a circle around me, not calling or writing people. Twenty milligrams no longer seemed to do the trick. Until I stabilized two months later, I took 30 mg. a day. Now I'm on 20 mg. a day once more.

With Prozac I may still have days of sadness, a low feeling, but I can still work and function and feel decent about myself and life. The extreme edge of pain is soothed and everything seems possible. Without Prozac the pain is excruciating at times and a desire to just give up is rife. I know I'm feeling dreadful, behaving miserably. It scares me. Prozac takes that edge off; it compensates for whatever chemical imbalance I may have.

The pros for me of Prozac are that, except for the initial week or so and occasionally months into taking it, there are no side effects. I don't get fat, jittery, nervous, whatever. I'm me, just less in pain, able to lift myself above the depression (or at least to a shallower level).

The fact that I feel better about myself—and others have commented on it—makes the outrageous cost of the Prozac a necessary expense. I probably wouldn't still be here if it weren't for Prozac.

Gary Gaw, forty-four years old, is an aspiring singer-songwriter-musician who receives SSDI [Social Security disability insurance] due to substance abuse.

Depression runs in my entire family. I didn't understand why I was so sad compared to others. So, a life of hell began. Drugs, alcohol, jails, prison, but it only got worse. The longer I lived, the more intense the depression, and I realize the drugs and alcohol only aggravated the condition but at least I gained temporary peace.

I couldn't work, socialize, concentrate; I had no energy; I cried, felt hurt, lost my appetite, slept a lot, couldn't sleep—a living hell! I couldn't manage money at all. My sex life was sporadic—very seldom—and meaningless then, and I had no desire. I always kept up my appearance because I felt that was all I had.

I've been in more treatment centers than I care to discuss. After completing one treatment program, a doctor cared enough to dig into the unrealized problem. He put me on Sinequan [generic name: doxepin; tricyclic antidepressant], beginning at 75 mg. The depression eased somewhat but only temporarily. Eventually I was up to 250 mg. and very tired and sleepy all the time.

I have been assigned many different diagnoses: personality disorder, depressive disorder, acute depression, clinical depression, circumstantial depression, chemical imbalance. I have come to rest with inherited chemically imbalanced depression.

Well, I went on to see many other doctors, changing medications (and exploring my responses). There was Elavil (sleepy), Desyrel (headaches), Triavil (tired), Pamelor (nothing), Paxil (nervous), imipramine (felt strange), and, finally, Prozac. I knew I had to find something or die an abuser. Benzodiazepines [brand-name examples: Ativan, Klonopin, Valium; antianxiety drugs] helped, but I eventually built a tolerance and addiction to them.

At first Prozac made me restless. I had some trouble with an upset stomach, gas, frequent urination, perspiring more than usual, and gritting my teeth. After about a month the side effects lessened. I've been taking Prozac for six years (since its release) and I am much better. I began with 20 mg. in the morning and I now take 40 mg. in the morning and 20 mg. after lunch.

I'm working, going to church, socializing; I've got more energy, and I'm much more content. Yes, I still have bad days, but thank God, not every day. I sleep soundly, have no side effects. Prozac helps me be "the real me." I am not a believer in a magic pill; however, I feel Prozac has given me a balance to proceed with life as best I can. I spent much of my life mad at God. "Why," I asked God, "must I be so unhappy?" I've quit asking why—I thank Him for opportunities such as this to share my experiences.

You may ask, why begin with 20 mg. and move to take 60 mg. a day? I explained to my doctor after a year that I felt the Prozac wasn't as effective as it had been, thus the increase, and it helped. After four years on Prozac I began to feel very tired in the afternoon, thus the 20 mg. in the afternoon.

As I've said, I've been to many doctors, some liberal, some conservative, some somewhere in between. Every doctor has told me there is no tolerance level with Prozac. This I question. Should the 60 mg. cease to relieve most of my depression, then what?

So, in summary, today I'm doing just fine. I get some depression from time to time but, heck, who doesn't? The overall gloom and doom has subsided. I once was suicidal but no longer. I work, laugh, talk, exercise, eat well, feel pretty good. I know I am better and have been since Prozac. I thank God for peace of mind. And I thank Him for working through doctors and medicine. It's a godsend!

Peggy Barr works and plays in North Carolina.

I started taking 20 mg. of Prozac about two and a half years ago. I was having a great deal of trouble sleeping and had been on all sorts of sleeping pills for a year or more. A friend suggested I take Prozac. Her therapist prescribed it for her because she had not slept well most of her life. She said she took it for one month and started sleeping fine the whole night and stopped taking the Prozac and continued to sleep fine.

I called my doctor the next day and started taking it. It took right at one month to get the effects of it in my system, and I began sleeping great and continued to sleep great for six or eight months. Thinking everything was cured, I stopped taking it, but in about four weeks my sleep pattern started failing to let me sleep through the night. So I started back and within three or four weeks I was right back on schedule. And I have remained on it with no side effects whatsoever. Also I did lose about seven pounds at the start, and it has remained off.

I'd like to add that as a bonus, Prozac has helped me in another area. All my life I've had a problem with relationships, going from one to another, taking the rejection really bad. I had been in a relationship for five years, and all seemed fine until last January, when he left me, moved all his things out while I was at work. I slept that very night, which for me was a miracle. I even went to work the next day. Normally I would have been physically ill from depression.

The next week was my birthday and the next week was Valentine's. I cried off and on for two or three weeks, but basically I was okay. After about four weeks I ran a single's ad in the paper and started living again. Everyone who knows me and how I've handled these situations in the past can't believe how well I've done. I can't believe it either.

It is definitely the Prozac, no doubt in my mind. I've told many of my friends about its effects on my self-esteem and my moods. It is wonderful. I feel like a new person.

Karen Lesley lives in southern California. She loves her two daughters and hiking—she has climbed Mount Whitney—among other things.

From as far back as I can remember, I have been shy, sensitive, easily intimidated, and felt inferior because of it. I've always worried about what people would think and was afraid of being rejected or judged deficient.

After working for fifteen years for a school principal who was extremely critical and exacting, I was a candidate for a nervous breakdown. It seemed that the harder I tried, the worse things got. I could spend hours teaching at school and hours at home planning and preparing, and still be criticized. At an all-time physical and emotional low, I quit my job. I had started seeing a psychologist just months before quitting, and he gave me tremendous support through the resignation of my job and the emotional aftermath of the whole experience.

Two experiences stand out as illustrations of my state of mind during the last few years of my teaching job. Sometimes the stress would become especially heavy and a particular problem would arise at school that would cut me into pieces. I couldn't see a solution. I was in excruciating emotional pain. I remember driving down the freeway screaming this primeval scream until my throat was raw and there was nothing left. I wanted to drive off a cliff and be done with it, but being a mother of two little girls, I couldn't bring myself to leave them that way. I know the pain of losing someone you love to suicide, as my sister died by her own hand several years ago.

The second experience happened one Friday when a confrontation with a parent left me devastated. I knew I hadn't done anything wrong, yet I also knew I would receive no support from my principal. I came home an emotional wreck and told my husband to get packed because we were leaving for the weekend. We threw a few things in the motor home and drove off. All I remember from that weekend is the unending pain and the tears that wouldn't stop flowing. I laid in the back of the motor home as my husband drove and wished with all my heart that the motor home would float off into the sky and explode in the same fashion as the *Challenger,* leaving nothing behind but pieces of a broken, tormented life.

I ran into my sister-in-law in the grocery store during all this and we began talking. Something set me off and the tears started to flow. I couldn't stop them. Soon after this, she stopped by the house to see me, told me about her experience with Prozac, and suggested I go on it. She recognized the same characteristics in me that she had experienced before she began taking it. Prozac had helped her to feel normal again.

I have always steered clear of medications, being a believer in natural methods of healing. So I resisted using Prozac for several months. Later my psychologist would suggest I talk to my doctor about getting a prescription. Finally I decided to give it a try. I really had no idea what it could do for me. I didn't even think I was depressed anymore, although I still cried very easily and was still screaming at my sweet girls. Even after I began taking Prozac, I quit using it several times when I ran out of a prescription, only to realize that I wasn't coping very well without it.

When I first started Prozac, it upset my stomach slightly and made me feel a bit nauseated. I had a dry mouth and felt a tic inside my stomach, sort of a twitching or spastic feeling—like a tic you get in your eye. I knew it was from the Prozac because every time I would quit and begin again, the same side effects would appear. They never lasted long though, only a few days.

I also didn't recognize the good effects until I went off Prozac and back on again several times over a six-month period. The effects for me are immediate, although doctors say that it takes about two weeks for it to build up in your body and for you to feel the results. I feel better within a twenty-four- to forty-eight-hour period.

My uncontrolled crying stops. I feel confident, not so self-conscious, around people. I *BELIEVE* that they will like me, a real contrast to the way I felt before. I don't scream at my kids. I can think faster and words come to mind when I need them instead of having to search constantly for the right word, and feeling stupid when it won't surface. I realize that I have a tremendous vocabulary, because words that I didn't even know were part of my vocabulary come to mind at appropriate times.

Because I have no insurance coverage since quitting my job, I have to pay for my own medications. Prozac is quite expensive—seventy-five dollars for a month's supply—so I try to get samples from my doctor. Because my mother had samples of Zoloft that she gave me, I have been using it for about two months now. I have found that I have retained some of the good effects I had from Prozac and that I have lost some: my thinking has slowed, and I have transient moments of rejection sensitivity.

One disturbing side effect of Prozac is that I lose the ability to become sexually aroused after I've been on it for a while. On

Zoloft, this effect seems to disappear. Once in a great while I find myself thinking dark thoughts about dying. I attribute this to a lapse in the serotonin level in my brain a day or so after I forget to take the medication.

I can truthfully say that Prozac and Zoloft have changed my life. I find pleasure in living where before I had experienced only pain. Life is generally good these days.

Michael Stein is a thirty-three-year-old New Yorker who now lives in San Francisco.

I suffer from major depression with obsessive-compulsive disorder [OCD]. Beyond that, I have never been diagnosed formally, except that I'm "neurotic." People tell me I'm high-strung. I first started seeing shrinks when I was five and have been in therapy pretty consistently since then.

My second shrink replied, when I asked him about the possibility of my using psychotropic medication, that he "didn't believe in them." When I was in college, I learned that some of the newer antidepressants were used to treat OCD. The psychologist I was seeing said he didn't think I was someone who would benefit from taking them.

It was my fourth therapist (an MSW) [master's degree in social work] who suggested to me that an antidepressant probably would help me, by treating my insomnia. I had tried many other remedies for it: over-the-counter drugs, various herbs, amino acids, relaxation tapes; the one other prescription medication I had tried was Halcion [generic name: triazolam; short-acting sedative], which worked for a week, then stopped having an effect on me. Perhaps an antidepressant would help me sleep and affect the other symptoms of my depression.

I did see a psychiatrist who gave me a prescription for Norpramin [generic name: desipramine; tricyclic antidepressant]. I took it for two years, with improved sleep, improved recovery from low or depressed periods, and fewer depressive episodes.

After I moved to San Francisco I happened to read several magazine articles that mentioned Prozac and other newer antidepressants had been shown to be helpful in treating OCD. I approached my psychiatrist with the idea of trying one of these medications. He gave me the choice of taking either Prozac or Anafranil [generic name: clomipramine; tricyclic antidepressant]. I decided on Anafranil because it would probably turn out to be less expensive than Prozac and because of our mutual concern that Prozac might make me more anxious and tense than I already was. The Anafranil was indeed successful in treating my OCD. I still obsessed but much less often than previously. In addition, many of my compulsive habits (e.g., if I touched the right side of my face, I had to touch the left side) slipped away.

Before I took Norpramin I had had a grand mal seizure, which was never explained because I had no neurological problems. After I started taking Anafranil, a neurologist determined I no longer needed phenobarbitol [brand names: Barbita, Solfoton; antiepileptic; barbiturate], and I discontinued taking it. Within the first year and a half of taking Anafranil, I had three more grand mal seizures. My neurologist learned that a side effect of Anafranil is seizures in people who have a history of them.

In March 1993, I started taking Prozac. Unlike the Norpramin or Anafranil, Prozac did not give results from the day I first took it. I started taking 20 mg. per day and built up to 80 mg. per day, which is what I take at present. The dose the psychiatrist recommended originally was 60 mg., but at that dose I was still depressed.

I was surprised that it was okay for me to take more than one 20 mg. pill because of the articles I've read. One of the advantages touted about Prozac over earlier antidepressants, such as the tricyclics, is the ease with which it's dispensed: everyone always takes one capsule a day. My shrink said that while one capsule a day is often sufficient for treating simple depression, three or four are usually necessary for OCD.

After I increased the dose to 80 mg. per day, my depression and OCD were as much under control as when I was taking Anafranil. The only undesirable side effect I've experienced is that when I'm having sex or masturbating, I sometimes have difficulty ejaculating. One woman I was involved with for a while was frustrated by this. But, eventually, I do ejaculate. All things with time. I consider this only a minor problem.

One side effect that I am happy to be experiencing is that I have lost twenty pounds since starting on it (a six-month period at this writing). I am now close to the weight I would like to be. People have told me, "You look great! You've lost a lot of weight!" and I especially like that. I think part of the reason for the weight loss is that the Prozac has cut my appetite and the other part is that the medication has increased my metabolic rate and, therefore, I burn calories faster.

Norah Zilisch is thirty-one years old and lives in Wisconsin. Her favorite hobby is training dogs—for agility competition and, as a private teacher, for obedience and manners.

I've been taking Prozac for almost two years now, and I believe that it has saved my life. While that may sound drastic, it's true. I had been in therapy for ten years, but no matter what positive steps I took, I couldn't shake the feeling that I was only a shell of a person and would never be at peace with myself.

I never was an outgoing person. I preferred to keep to myself. I read to escape whatever I couldn't face, and somehow made it through college and got a teaching job in New Mexico. I left after one year and moved to Los Angeles, where I lived and taught for two years. I also met the man who is now my husband. It was while I lived there that I first noticed feeling down and lonely. As time went on my bad days stretched into weeks, and as the feelings lasted longer, they intensified. I moved to Wisconsin, married, and thought I had left despair behind. That was not the case, and soon depression affected every facet of my life.

I started with a counselor, mostly for marital problems. I clearly remember that last depression before I took medication. It was November 1992. My husband and I were on the edge, and I felt so very empty and alone. I went to a teachers' convention and ran into one of my best friends. I greeted her like a zombie. She became very angry with me, and I hated her for that. But she didn't understand.

It took longer than usual for me to awaken from the darkness. When I did, it was crystal-clear to me that I wouldn't survive another episode. I vowed to do whatever I had to do to get help. I started taking Prozac the next week.

When I first started taking the medication, I only noticed the side effects: dry mouth, feeling like I was getting a cold, and nausea. I just couldn't eat much. That was okay with me, though. I ended up losing some weight, which has since returned. The dry mouth didn't last very long either.

I told only three people about taking the medication, and asked them to tell me if they noticed any differences in me. After about four weeks I noticed the difference. I laughed, had fun, relaxed. I loved Christmas for the first time. I got along with my whole family. It was incredible!

The specter of despair still hung in my mind, as I felt that it couldn't be gone that quickly. But as Christmas vacation ended, I felt down. That's all. Down, sad, blue. Not empty, suicidal, wretched. And the feeling had a reason; it wasn't some cloud of unknown origin. And it left. Quietly.

I was amazed, and still am. Last Christmas I ran out of Prozac and was short on money. I started taking it every other day, if I remembered. Soon I was out of Prozac but had all my Christmas presents bought. I now know the best present for my family and myself is to keep taking the medication. It was a lesson for me, one I suppose I needed to learn. The depressed feelings came back with more force than even I could believe. I was very afraid, and it took every ounce of strength to hold myself together.

I'll take Prozac until the day I die, if it will keep my brain functioning correctly. Sometimes I have to remind myself that it's a chemical problem in my brain. That it's not me, or who I am.

In the past few months I've become more focused and outgoing. I'm getting involved in the things I care about. I'm even focusing on my teaching career a little. I make plans and follow through on them. And my relationship with my husband is peaceful. We still argue, but there is no desperation for me anymore. I don't know if this is a direct result of the drug or a result of my own satisfaction that my life is so much better now. And I don't really care.

Bob Millwood lives in North Carolina.

I was sexually and physically abused as a teenager.

And I slowly was slipping into a deep, dark hole of hopelessness and despair. I chose to be hospitalized, fearing that my thoughts of suicide would result in the actual taking of my own life. I was a self-mutilator as well—my way of punishing myself for my abuse and for feeling so horribly depressed.

In the hospital I was placed on antianxiety drugs and antidepressants. The first was desipramine [trade name: Norpramin; tricyclic antidepressant], suggested by my doctor. I was willing to try anything. I thought it would lift my depression immediately. *WRONG!* It took two weeks for the drug to take hold and for results to start happening. Desipramine made me feel tired and I had a big increase in appetite. I also had a dry mouth, so I found myself drinking liquids a lot. I hated the side effects, especially the weight gain, and I asked to be taken off almost right away. But my doctor recommended I stay on it for a month.

I did stay on it for his recommended time. But at the end of the month I asked for a new antidepressant and was switched to Elavil [generic name: amitriptyline; tricyclic antidepressant]. After the first dose of this I slept all day and I refused to take this drug any longer.

Then I was switched to Prozac. After my last two antidepressants I asked about side effects. It was told to me by my doctor that the side effects were almost minimal and I should experience more energy. It sounded good and, best of all, no sleeping and only one pill a day. After a week I did experience headaches, but Motrin or Tylenol seemed to make it tolerable. After a month of taking the Prozac, I lost the ten pounds I'd gained from the other drugs. It was like a miracle had taken place.

Before my drug therapy, I had trouble concentrating; my thoughts were only filled with suicide. I had no energy, I wasn't motivated to do anything, and I truly wanted to just disappear from the face of the earth.

I stayed on Prozac for a year and a half. And through therapy and good drug therapy management, I was able to get off Prozac after two years of being on it.

Dawn White is a twenty-seven-year-old Utah resident. She enjoys playing racquetball with her husband, sleeping under the stars, and hanging out with her younger brother.

"Have you at least considered taking an antidepressant?" my hospital social worker earnestly asked. The look in her eyes gave me reason to think she was hoping for my recovery as much as I was. I had already been approached on this issue by my therapist, as well as by the psychiatrist she consulted. Ten years of battling anorexia and bulimia had really taken a toll on me, and they could see it.

Although I knew they all meant well, the concept of control was a major issue for me. The thought of putting a drug in my body that could control my behavior was out of the question. *People who have to take drugs are weak and probably crazy. I am neither. I can do it on my own!*

To outsiders who had seen my weight go as low as seventy-two pounds, I'm sure the thought of me rejecting a medication that could possibly help save my life was unbelievable. I knew I needed help badly—but I didn't need drugs! *I will go in the hospital, take some time out, and I will be okay.* After two weeks of inpatient care, I realized this was obviously not the case. I still had the same urges, desires, and unhappiness.

What is wrong with me? Where is this all coming from? I remembered once seeing my grandma take pills she described to me as helping her "not worry so much." *Maybe there is something genetically wrong with me and not my fault at all.* Finally I conceded to try Prozac despite the fear I had of being out of control. The first pill I took brought back memories of a co-worker telling me his wife, who was on Prozac, had gained quite a bit of weight. I panicked. I asked for a list of side effects from the hospital pharmacist. Surprisingly, a potential side effect was anorexia. *Maybe I can lose weight by taking this drug.* I continued to take 20 mg. daily.

The first two to three weeks I didn't really notice any changes. I asked the psychiatrist for more. He prescribed 40 mg. per day for my eighty-pound frame. I noticed sometimes that I was light-headed but attributed it to my eating problem. I had a difficult time sleeping, was still purging almost daily, and seemed to be losing weight. I did feel a bit of an energy boost I hadn't felt before, which helped me get through each day at work.

This energy boost made me think if I took three pills, I would be even better off. I talked to the psychiatrist and he told me to try it. I did but immediately returned to two pills per day. The costs of the light-headedness and dizziness weren't worth the possible increase in energy for me.

After two or three months of taking 40 mg. per day, I noticed myself being more extroverted. I began seeking out others rather than isolating myself. The dark cloud I felt I had been under was lifting and even turning gray instead of black and bleak. I began noticing things I hadn't before, like the fact that I had caring friends and family all around me. I began reaching out to them.

While at a store with one of my "newfound" friends six to seven months after taking 40 mg. per day, I had a grand mal seizure and was rushed to the hospital. I woke up four days later to find out I had experienced two grand mal seizures, not just one. I was told all the tests indicated the cause of the seizures to be unknown. However, the emergency-room doctor was appalled at the amount of Prozac I had been taking with such a low body weight; I was shocked to hear Prozac lowered my seizure threshold. She decreased my dosage to one 20 mg. tablet per day and added Dilantin [generic name: phenytoin; anticonvulsant drug] for seizure control.

Within two weeks I was back to work full-time. One month later I had another seizure while at work. Once again I was taken to the hospital. The emergency-room team found my Dilantin level too low. I was given intravenous seizure medication and released the same day. I realized at that point if I wanted to keep taking Prozac, I needed to make sure my Dilantin level was stable. Purging created havoc on it. This practice would have to be discontinued.

Prozac, coupled with a stable Dilantin level, seemed to help me be more able to focus, concentrate, and to open up to others. I was beginning to gain weight and was able to deal with it better than ever before. I began feeling I could actually be worthwhile. I still had the desire to binge and purge but was better able to talk myself out of it. Prozac was by no means the cure for me but rather a tool to help me access other tools and supports—God, family, friends, support groups, dietitian, therapist—to aid in my recovery. A new twist had been given to my thoughts. Prozac gave me that little nudge toward action.

Today I weigh around one hundred and five pounds and take 40 mg. of Prozac per day. I feel energetic, more peaceful, and more optimistic about my future. Sometimes I feel jittery and have difficulty sleeping, but it's not anything harmful to me. I can now genuinely laugh and smile. I am not as afraid as I used to be to talk to new people and have even taken the opportunity to speak to women about eating disorders. Because I feel better about myself and stronger inside, I have been able to accept a marriage proposal from a wonderful man I previously felt I didn't deserve to be with. This fall I am beginning course work toward a master's degree at a local university, while working full-time—a task of which two years ago I would have thought myself incapable.

Although I know Prozac isn't a miracle drug, I have no intention of giving it up. Sometimes I still purge, yet it's nothing like before—I am much more able to get back on track. As long as I keep my Dilantin level on target, I can assume I will have no more seizures. It is my belief that Prozac has helped me access the courage and strength I have inside to push ahead and make necessary changes in my life. Prozac didn't change my life but rather helped me help myself.

Denise Williams lives in California.

"I can't take it anymore, I just can't take it anymore." This was my predominant thought month in and month out, over at least twenty years of my life. As I glance back through the personal journals I've maintained, I see the patterns and themes were always the same: life was a living hell. I don't recall how it all began, I remember about the time I was seventeen or eighteen, I began to experience some real dark moods. All I could think of was killing myself, ending the tormented feelings. In my mid- to late twenties I realized that a lot of these feelings happened around my menstrual cycle. My doctor eventually took me off the Pill, thinking maybe the hormones were wreaking havoc on my system. I can remember feeling like there was some hope, but it was short-lived, the terrible dark moods continued.

By the time I was thirty years old, I had been hospitalized and treated for severe depression and had been in therapy for several years. I was only on Elavil [generic name: amitriptyline; tricyclic antidepressant] once for a short period of time. I remember it making me feel like a zombie, no highs or lows, just kind of flat. I managed to get back to a functional level—and to the outside world, I probably seemed very normal. The only ones who really knew that I had some emotional issues were my family, and my mother in particular. I think my sister and brother just thought I was in a consistently bad mood.

Over the years I began to see more and more information on what we now know as premenstrual syndrome [PMS]. Although my hormone and thyroid levels did vary during my cycle, there were never any extreme readings. Still I was convinced that I had PMS and ended up trying every conceivable form of treatment, from healthy diet and exercise to synthetic hormones.

I began to seek out specialists in the area, gathering all the information I could. Some months were better than others, but the depressions had not gone away. I can remember having to make up excuses to leave work many times, feeling like I could explode at any moment. The closer I got to my period, the more I begin to notice intense amounts of anger building up, just general anger at anything in my way. I used to call myself Dr. Jekyll and Mr. Hyde, because I seemed to have two very distinct personalities.

About three years ago I went into a deep depression right before the Christmas holidays. The holidays were always very hard for me, but I spent this one away from my family and in bed. I held on for a few more months and convinced myself that prayer would get me through it. I even resumed therapy in hopes of a quick release.

The depression didn't go away, and on Easter Sunday I decided to go to church but realized that I couldn't get out of the bed. I had been in touch with my mother and she knew I was going through a bad spell, but I don't think either of us realized how bad off I was. The next day the well opened. I started crying, but then realized that I was no longer crying but weeping and screaming. I had just enough sanity left to make the appropriate calls to my insurance company and get myself admitted.

I stayed in the hospital for about nine days, which at the time gave me a chance to pull myself together. My doctor started me on Prozac, but it seemed to take about the whole hospital stay to take effect. In that time I also did a lot of talking to the psychiatrist and was able to get some additional insights into what may have been compounding my depressions. It wasn't the first time that I had had to get in touch with some of my childhood issues, and wouldn't be the last. By the time I was released from the hospital, I again felt like there was some hope for me.

But the first few days out of the hospital were overwhelming. For one thing the Prozac had my heart racing so fast my doctor had to prescribe some Xanax [generic name: alprazolam; antianxiety drug] to calm me down. I was starting to feel disenchanted, like maybe things weren't going to work out. Over the next few days, I found it hard to get grounded, like something else was working against me.

Although I returned to work within another week, I could still feel a tremendous emptiness inside. I started to go into the conference room to cry for a few minutes at a time. I knew then that the worst wasn't over. By then my mother had stepped into the picture and tried to convince me to take some time off of work and get rehospitalized. At first I resisted—I had just come out without any relief—but over the next few days I realized that this was going to be a reality.

I managed to get admitted to a hospital in southern California close to my mother and family. I ended up staying there for one month, and in that time I was again started on Prozac. This time, I had a reaction to it that made my eyelids puff up. This went on for about two weeks. Interestingly enough, this still happens to me whenever I become too stressed, so I've begun to use it as an indicator for myself.

I did notice that the more I talked, the better I felt. The program was very comprehensive so that after that first month I began to feel a lot better. After I was released, I stayed with my mother for a few additional weeks so that I could continue in the hospital program on an outpatient basis.

It's been about three years since that experience, and I have been on Prozac ever since. I hear a lot about how it's changed people's lives, and I guess it did change mine. I haven't had a depression since that time. Oh sure, I still get down now and then, but it's more in the normal range, no extremes. My self-image seems to have improved, and I've had time to explore other issues without feeling devastated by them.

I think I experienced a euphoric feeling when I had been on Prozac for about a month, and in comparison with where I had been, I probably was euphoric. Now I just feel normal, which still has a lot of daily variations. This is the way I've always dreamt of feeling. My relationships with my friends and family have vastly improved. I no longer have to hide those parts of myself that were hurting so bad.

At first, I was really afraid to get on a medication that I would need to take every day, plus I knew my insurance plan didn't want to cover the costs, but now I'm just thankful that it works. I have tried to reduce the dosage but every time I get to less than 10 mg. a day, I begin to notice mood swings again, so I'm still at 20 mg. a day.

I have faced the reality that I may need to take Prozac for many years to come. Besides not knowing any long-term side effects (especially since I still want to have a baby), I feel very comfortable with my decision to continue on it. I find that I am more comfortable with it than my family and friends. I think they still wish that I could function without this "drug." But I wake each day feeling that life is very much worth living, and *that's* reason enough for me!

Sarah Brodsky is a proud seventy-nine-year-old mother and grandmother who lives in Maryland.

In December 1992, I had a triple bypass heart operation done in Washington. I was admitted to the local hospital very frequently that winter due to various troubles, one of which is emphysema, and I became very depressed. My doctor prescribed Prozac. My daughter objected because of the drug's reputation, but the doctor insisted, so I took it. I trusted my doctor totally; I felt when he held my hand he could heal me.

This medication left me in such a debilitated state, both mentally and physically. My daughter had to take care of everything for me. I lost my appetite and went from 167 pounds to 112 pounds. I was afraid to take a bath or shower—even to wash my hair. Everything frightened me. I reverted to childhood. I couldn't even walk. My last hospitalization was for eleven weeks. I had pulmonary edema and serious heart failure and was not expected to survive.

My daughter and I complained to my doctor, suggesting that the Prozac weakened my system. But he insisted I continue taking Prozac. I refused, so he refused to continue to take care of me. I stopped and he stopped, but I'm the better for it just the same.

I have now [August 1994] a group of doctors and have started to gain weight—I'm up to 126 pounds—and have recently started taking care of my affairs. It has taken that long to recuperate.

Joshua Hadley lives with his cat, Rainbow, in a midwestern city. He edits, writes, dances, and plays music.

When I went on Prozac for the first time, I felt desperate, scared, pained, maybe close to the end of my life. I had already tried other antidepressants but was still searching for relief from years of depression and chronic pain that no one could adequately explain.

I'd first tried an antidepressant—imipramine [brand names: Tofranil, Janimine; tricyclic antidepressant]]—about ten years ago, when I was twenty-five. I felt stuck and depressed. I had a successful life by many standards: a good job, good pay, freedom to go where I wanted when I wanted. And yet I was floundering in emotional quicksand. I'd feel empty, then perhaps merely adequate, then empty again. In an apparently solid life was fluidity; in stability, nothing but unfulfilled expectations.

My psychotherapist referred me to a psychiatrist, who asked me why I was so depressed. I couldn't really say except that the world wasn't turning out as I'd expected. I left with a prescription for the imipramine. I took solace in the fact that it wasn't a dose for depression but for "anxiety." I recall hoping that the medication would save me. I quickly discovered that its main effects did not include salvation, but rather constipation, dry mouth, and difficulty in urinating, all of which made me feel worse. I tried to get used to the drug, but because of the side effects, I eventually said "Enough."

Shortly thereafter, I was diagnosed and treated for cancer, lost my sister to suicide, and hurt my back—all in one year. I realize now that the cancer and my sister's death were much more devastating than I could allow myself to comprehend at the time. Such events exposed me to loss—of the body, of health, of strength, of love, of the earnest hope of the world as a nurturing place. Perhaps if I had been able at the time to confront fully my feelings of rage and hurt (as I've since been doing), I wouldn't have needed to take Prozac. But I buried those feelings as deep as I could, and so my body gave me something I couldn't ignore: chronic, disabling back pain.

I turned my attention to finding a solution to the physical pain. Unfortunately, several years, a few painkillers, a few more tricyclics, and bunches of doctors and physical therapists later, I felt unable to adequately control the pain or cope with my life. So I quit my job, sold many of my belongings, and moved a thousand miles into my parents' home. The anxiety-riddled depression returned full force, sinking into me under the weight of feelings that I'd failed, that I'd limp-wristedly given up. I believed I'd moved home to die.

I soon received my Prozac prescription from an internist at a pain clinic. While I wanted relief from the depression, I preferred to think I was taking the Prozac more to boost my body's levels of serotonin so I wouldn't experience as much pain, which had begun mysteriously to affect other areas of my body.

Within a week of starting Prozac, I began feeling jittery and even more anxious, sensations that got worse before they got better. (I also felt nauseated, a symptom that faded without any prolonged treatment.) At varying times, I took two different medications to counteract the extremely uncomfortable and disturbing jitteriness. The first was Xanax [generic name: alprazolam; antianxiety drug]; later, the second time I went on Prozac, I took Desyrel [generic name: trazodone; serotonin agonist] at night to help me sleep.

After the month-long adjustment period, the drug seemed to begin working wonderfully, and I noticed rapid improvement in my mood. I remember driving along the street with my mother and saying how wonderful it was not to feel scared, for the first time in a very, very long time.

I believe that the Prozac helped me break through a wall of blackness that I previously had been unsuccessful doing. It helped me feel good enough to begin doing the real, hard work of changing through my ongoing psychotherapy.

In addition to feeling freer, safer, and happier, or perhaps because of these feelings, I began to do more. I took classes in the creative arts, began dancing, had a short story accepted for publication, started my own business, began volunteering extensively. Eventually, I moved out of my parents' house.

The only prolonged unpleasant side effect I noticed from Prozac was sexual. I seemed to have a lower sex drive, and I found it took longer to have an orgasm when aroused. This sometimes felt uncomfortable, though I wouldn't call it a major side effect. It did, however, continue through the period of my use of the Prozac; it didn't wear off like the jitteriness. The benefits continued to be a lifting of the disabling depression, less physical pain, an increased sense of mastery of my life, and greater alertness and stamina.

It seems many people have heard about the danger of suicide while on Prozac. And yes, the first time I was on Prozac, I became suicidal. I'd felt like killing myself before, but I came closer than ever about seven months after being on Prozac. I collected the pills to do it, and I wrote a note. Just like my sister. I was ready.

I think it's important to emphasize that, in the end, I didn't do it. Having suicidal thoughts—even serious ones—is quite different from committing suicide. In retrospect, I think my thoughts of ending my life because I felt worthless were much more the result of the excruciatingly painful feelings I was experiencing (primarily through psychotherapy) than it was because of the Prozac.

It's possible that I may have killed myself had I not started Prozac. It is giving Prozac too much credit to say that it causes suicide. Suicide, for me, was and is about existence and the passion of living. It isn't about a bad drug. Sometimes, in fact, I am struck with devastating sadness that Prozac and its later relatives were not available for my sister in her deepest despair that led to her suicide. I can't know whether it would have helped her. But I'm drawn to the thought that Prozac could have given her more of a chance, as it did for me.

Each time I went off the Prozac, it seemed to take about six weeks to get out of my system. As it left my body, I noticed I had a little less energy, a little more anxiety. The first time I went off, I began experiencing a series of chronic pain episodes after about six weeks. They didn't abate, so a few months later, my internist and I decided to try antidepressants again. She suggested Zoloft, which she said would work faster and wear off faster, and had potentially even fewer side effects than Prozac. I didn't experience myself as depressed when I began the Zoloft, just in need of another boost of serotonin to help with the pain.

That I responded very poorly to the Zoloft frightened me. I had so many side effects that I had to stop within a week, and started the Prozac again. I had to go through an adjustment period again, but I knew what to expect and how to manage it, so it didn't seem so bad.

As I write this, I've been off Prozac for five months. The two previous times I was on it, I had stopped taking it by simply stopping. Before I stopped Prozac this time, I reduced the standard dosage of 20 mg. daily to every other day, and then every third day. So when I finally stopped, I had a relatively small amount of the drug in my body.

Sometimes I still hurt, in mind and body, and feel less energetic than I would like. Since the last of the Prozac has left my bloodstream, I have sometimes awakened in the morning feeling depressed and anxious, or have developed pain that's hard to explain. When that happens, I'm tempted to think it's the old days all over again.

But in the six years since I've been on and off Prozac, I've learned a great deal about my emotional life, and about how intricately my physical pain was, and is, bound up with my emotions—particularly anger and anxiety. Using resources I've found within myself, particularly the awareness and appropriate expression of anger, I've learned that my pain, physical and emotional, can be reduced without medication.

I've learned that it is absolutely essential that I allow myself to be angry, to fume, to be pissed off, and if necessary, to say so. I've learned that effectively dealing with the depression and pain is about allowing myself to be myself: different, eccentric, bold, shy, clear, inconsistent. Whatever is there. Whatever it takes.

I realize that Prozac did not cure me. But it did help teach me what feeling good can be like. The rest, I've decided, is up to me.

Sometimes I'm sure I'll never need Prozac again. Sometimes I'm sure I will. The rest of the time I'm not sure at all. But I would like to know my unmedicated self fully. The best I can do, today, is to take the education Prozac helped provide and run with it, as far and as passionately—though not necessarily as fast—as I can.

ZOLOFT

[generic name: sertraline; selective serotonin reuptake inhibitor (SSRI); second-generation antidepressant with a shorter half-life than Prozac: 25 hours; therapeutic dose range: 50–200 mg. per day; FDA approved 1992]

Anne Morrison, who has lived in southern California for twenty-seven years, is a deacon in the Episcopal Church. She is very happily married and the mother of two grown children.

I am in the process of recovering from my third and most severe episode of depression. In looking back over the past two and a half years, I want to conclude either that I am a very slow learner or that recovery from depression is not a simple, straightforward process. Returning to health has been a complex weaving together of good medicine, psychotherapy, and stress management. I also must be willing to continually understand how my daily activities affect my mental health and make adjustments in those activities, when necessary. My most difficult challenge has been to admit that I am not without limitations and cannot do everything I want to. To recognize and make allowances for my weakness or limitation was harder than living in the blackness and despair of depression.

Although I have dealt with each depressive episode differently, they all arose in similar situations, presented the same symptoms, and required similar responses to ensure a return to health and normality—whatever that is. Clinical depression occurred when I had greatly overcommitted myself. In each situation I had taken on more and more work because I thoroughly enjoyed what I was doing. To make matters worse, I was spending nearly all my time talking with people, helping them to learn to solve their problems or live with their current circumstances—and yet, I am an introvert. I was allowing myself zero quiet and solitary time to get reenergized.

Depression occurred, then, when I had used up all my inner energy reserves and had been running on empty for many months. The symptoms of depression did not seem to come slowly. My memory is of a sudden change from one day to the next! My sunny world was dark, nearly black. I was exhausted with living and wanted to quit—I'd done it, and enough was enough. Death seemed a welcome event. I couldn't find the words to talk; I couldn't think or remember things. I wanted to sleep all day, but sleep at night was nearly impossible.

During the first depression, I managed to leave somewhat gracefully my jobs as volunteer coordinator and part-time manager of a new homeless shelter. I returned to school and began work on an advanced degree in theology. Continual contact with people was over, and a life of mostly quiet study had begun. Professional help during this time was solely from a psychotherapist. After six months of weekly visits, the depression had abated and I had learned new ways to think about myself and the choices I could make.

Five years later, however, when I began a second period of depression, I wanted another person to verify that what I was experiencing was indeed depression. I visited a recommended psychiatrist, who agreed not only that depression was my problem but believed that I was in a deeper depression than I realized. He recommended that I reestablish contact with my therapist and prescribed Prozac. I had heard about antidepressants and wasn't opposed to trying them.

After only ten days of very small doses, I panicked because of the extremely bizarre and indescribable emotions I was experiencing. We stopped the Prozac immediately and started with Zoloft. Relief! After about three weeks I was back to a nearly normal work schedule, and I began to entertain the possibility that life might be worth something after all.

After three months I could sleep at night, enjoy short conversations. Home chores were fairly easy, but everything still seemed a huge hurdle to jump over, and I had to think twice before I could convince myself to go for it. There were no side effects from the Zoloft, except a slight dampening of sexual desire. My therapist helped to counteract all the negative, self-deprecatory feelings that were a lingering part of my depression, and was teaching me stress-management skills.

I used Zoloft for two years, feeling better every month. I felt so good that I stopped seeing my therapist, cut back on the medication, and saw the psychiatrist only every three months. There were a few down periods lasting three to five days, but overall my energy level increased, and I felt I was back to my old healthy and energetic self.

Two months later, I crashed. In a six-hour period I sank into a darkness that separated me from everything. I had used Zoloft not as an aid to recovery but as a tool to allow me to push beyond my limits, so that the third episode of depression was far worse than either of the other two. I had not heard the warnings of both my doctor and therapist. Because of my stubborn insistence on jumping into too much activity, the psychiatrist suggested that I stop taking Zoloft and try Effexor [generic name: venlafaxine; new-generation antidepressant].

Living—with or without antidepressants—is complicated. It is the weaving together of separate threads into a strong fabric. I have to choose continually the threads that work best together. The antidepressant is a temporary thread, needed for a while to firm up the base until other threads of choice and care and nurture can weave a strong pattern of their own. With or without antidepressants, it is ultimately up to me to understand and manage my strengths and weaknesses and make choices to maintain a full and healthy life.

Ellen hails from New England and is a single, professional woman in her mid-forties.

Before Zoloft found its way to me at the age of forty-five, I was very self-destructive and rapidly turning suicidal. I had actually started weaving out of my lane on the highway while commuting in the hope other cars would hit me and I would have physical pain to focus on. I come from a personal and family history of substance abuse, including my taking LSD in the mid-sixties as a young college student; divorced, alcoholic parents; and an extended family of what I consider cultists—Christian Science adherents and Masons.

I always wondered why my alcoholic father hated to get to know me and my soon-to-become-alcoholic mother neglected to get to know me. I had hyper-self-consciousness in grammar school and high school, which intensified as I made my way in the world. Despite high educational achievements, I remained fearful and anxious, turning to an existential depression in order to abate the fear that degenerated rapidly into a deeper and physically based depression.

I stopped alcohol and cigarette abuse but soon had an unexpected mental breakdown. As a result, I began cognitive psychotherapy. One week after release from the private hospital ward, I found my symptoms were returning. They seemed to be physically based, so I began Pamelor [generic name: nortriptyline; tricyclic antidepressant]. Pamelor gave me vascular difficulties and heart palpitations. I was never able to tolerate the recommended dosage, but could tolerate the dosage for adolescents. I seemed to get better, probably due in part to continued substance-abuse abstinence.

But events and people began to trigger strong dysfunctional reactions in me, which, after more psychotherapy, convinced me I needed to change from Pamelor to Klonopin [generic name: clonazepam; antianxiety drug]. I liked it a lot better than the Pamelor. My mind seemed clearer, not being plagued by the intense anxiety I had become accustomed to. Klonopin alleviated autonomic nervous system symptoms, such as involuntary stomach muscle spasms before sleep.

I even thought I was "cured" and went off it. But I resumed taking it when suicidal and destructive urges worsened. My psychic angst was intensifying, to the point I wanted my brain to explode. Therapy wasn't helping. I became flippant, anhedonic, and rapidly psychotic; what may once have been drug hallucinations now were psychotic visions. I was a jerk at work but didn't know it.

Reluctant to take drugs, I yet sought out a psychiatrist. He mentioned the SSRIs. A good friend had a love-hate relationship with Prozac, while two other friends—Christians, yet!—were in love with Zoloft. I opted for Zoloft. From the first pill, after only fifteen minutes or so, I felt a tingling in my brain. I felt relaxed. The contented feeling increased. I laughed at my sardonic thought: it was a placebo effect I felt; because the shrink believed I was suicidal, he prescribed *any* medication to stop the suicide thoughts. The next day I looked for my friend Misery before taking the second pill. But I was looking through a glass darkly: Where was he? Down went the pill.

Life got better much quicker. So quickly I couldn't keep track of what happened when. I got my appetite back. I had no more insomnia. I smiled once in a while. I was not in a fog of psychic pain when I woke up on dark January mornings to get ready for work. I laughed at TV once in a while. I began to read again. People at work looked less like the ogres some of them are. They saw me smile and backed away in surprise. I thought no more of suicide. I was able to ask God to forgive me for telling him off in four-letter words—and I was able to hear Him say He would. I became bolder in expressing myself and communicating, and I had less self-consciousness interacting with others (particularly those of the opposite sex).

I suffer absolutely no side effects. Arguably, there is a measure of diarrhea, but I do not attribute it to the drug. I love it. I fear going off. I will try, but won't feel bad if I have to go back on.

I am still going strong. I feel that I am able, finally, to grow up from when I got stunted, the age I began taking drugs and ruining my ability to think for myself. What I notice most, and appreciate most, is my ability to suffer pain without running away. I have bought a stuffed animal to hug and that helps a lot, too. I have become more rational, if only because my emotions are not rampantly interfering with my thought processes. To others this may be elemental, but to me it is a matter of survival.

Toni is a forty-year-old, single white woman.

I've been fighting depression almost as long as I can remember, at least since junior high. In the worst periods, sometimes lasting months or even a few years, I would sleep long hours, usually during the day; miss appointments, skip classes or work, and be late everywhere I went; experience diminished appetite; have trouble concentrating or completing tasks and become easily confused; and experience extreme self-hatred, as if my worst enemy had taken up residence in my head. My sex drive seems to increase, as part of a general craving for physical comfort. In light of a poor self-image (and consequent inability to perceive myself as lovable or desirable), sexual tension in depressed periods is relieved through fantasies of degradation and humiliation, which of course reinforce the poor self-image.

I had tried a few medications over the years that were either of limited effectiveness or had intolerable side effects. In April 1992 I began taking Zoloft. It took several months of experimentation to find a dosage level that was effective without severe side effects. For a little over two years I have been taking 50 mg. daily. During that time I have had two primary side effects, both tolerable: occasional mild diarrhea and weight loss of fifteen to twenty pounds from my pre-Zoloft weight.

On the plus side, my energy is up; I can concentrate well enough to organize and complete tasks of some complexity, improving my ability to find and keep employment; I seem to interact better with others, empathizing with their situation while having enough distance to respond rationally; my appetite and sex drive (while still subject to ups and downs) are more stable than before; and I sleep less but still soundly. Except for one little, persistent symptom, I would pronounce Zoloft a miracle cure.

That symptom? I hate myself and wish I were dead.

In a way, Zoloft has made my life more of a living hell than before. Since being medicated, I now see very clearly that suicide is not an option because of the extreme pain it would inflict on my family. After two suicide attempts (pre-Zoloft), I also know that I don't really have the guts to go through with it (that line about suicide being "the coward's way out" is dangerous, propagandistic crap). And so I'm trapped in a life alone, unlovable, in great mental and emotional pain, with no hope of relief.

So what do I do? When I can, I try to fight off bad feelings by exercising, cooking and eating a good healthy meal, reading a book or going to a movie (I have a degree in film, and watching movies used to be my great passion). It gets harder and harder to force myself to do these things as I no longer feel much joy in doing them, and they seem at best a temporary palliative. So mostly I ignore the bad feelings, trusting they will eventually, if temporarily, subside. It's a bit like living with a tantrum-throwing toddler.

What I don't do is seek professional help, except for med checks. Psychiatrists have nothing to offer me but more or different medications that can only do more of the same. Indeed, after ticking off their list of quantifiable indicators (sleep, libido, appetite, ability to hold down a job with medical benefits), they seem at a loss to understand why I don't declare myself cured. Psychologists and other talking therapists seem

for the most part enamored of thc approach usually labeled cog-
nitive or rational emotive therapy. I have found this approach not only ineffective but dangerous. In fact, it was the method used by both the therapists who were treating me when I made my two suicide attempts.

Melissa Woodall hails from Texas, where her hobbies include drinking coffee and going to queer cinema. She holds an A.A. degree in general nonsense and is finishing her B.A.

I'm thirty-five today and the mountain can't get any higher. It's a big pile of shale that I've been climbing all my life, sliding down all my way up. If I hadn't let myself start on antidepressant medicine, I would have given up when I was thirty-four. I would have fallen off the mountain, my broken body lying in a heap at the bottom somewhere.

In therapy I had been talking and remembering and grieving and seething, but could not keep a positive, forward momentum in my head.

"We might think about medication," the doctor said. Nix to that fix—I resisted. I had been stoned for ten years. After quitting on my own, I was proud of being clearheaded, sharp-eyed, and clean. It was the crazy part I didn't like.

"You were self-medicating for a reason. How about trying a drug that will help you?" said the doctor kindly, meaning "Don't be an idiot, you can't do this on your own." I couldn't lift off generations of repression, hate, and self-loathing. I could not bring myself out of depression. And just as the body needs attention in sickness, the pain in my soul needed medicine.

Once I got over my invented trauma of being a drug addict again, I had to face my reluctance at being identified as a trendy Prozac zombie. So I took Zoloft and kept it a secret.

Referring to antidepressants as "St. Joseph's aspirin for the inner child" was about as trendy as I was willing to go. I knew not to let on how sick I was. I got the message that the general masses can't admit to mental distress, theirs or anyone else's, and certainly not as legitimate illness. If there isn't a cast to sign or a sneeze to say God bless after, the suffering isn't real. It shamed me into silence about how much Zoloft was helping me.

I got over that feeling, too. Soon I wanted to tell everyone how good I felt.

"Have you noticed anything different about me lately?" I asked my roommate, a woman on the top of my hit list for her housekeeping sins.

"Yeah. You seem more open, lighter, happier." She said this with a smile, perhaps knowing of her narrow escape.

I was happy. It was amazing to me how a small pill could change me in ways I thought were impossible. I could go to sleep with the blues and wake up singing "Oklahoma!" I tried to plunge myself into a bad mood because, after all, that is what I was used to. I succeeded only in giving myself a headache.

The doctor couldn't explain what was changing in my head. The closest she got was showing me a visual aid about serotonin that a pharmaceutical company had left with her. It was one of those underwater drop-the-ball-in-the-hole toys parents give to their kids on long car trips. I annoyed the good doctor for a while playing with it, asking "why?" and "how?" Finally, exasperated, she said, "There might be side effects."

Aside from some farting and a month of dizziness, I had very few problems adjusting to the chemicals in my body. I did, however, create a physical problem for myself by combining lots of caffeine with my morning Zoloft. It gave me the kind of speed rush that I liked so much when I was doing crystal meth. My self-induced side effects were heart palpitations, a trip to the doctor for an EKG, and my psychiatrist taking me off the antidepressant for a month.

I scared myself silly, and now I behave, because the withdrawal from the Zoloft was a major backward roller-coaster ride in dizziness. After a week, I thought the head plunges were going away, but they only changed direction. I began to experience sideways dizziness, something I never thought possible.

I had been worried about my life without Zoloft. It didn't help that a friend had begged me not to start taking antidepressants—she claimed they would mask what was causing my depression, and when I stopped, life would be hard again. Fortunately, I was also experiencing a new ability to handle life. My down moods were short-lived and didn't spiral out of control into darkness anymore.

I am happy to announce from the battlefront that antidepressants are like LSD: it depends on where your head is before you make the trip. It takes a lot of honest self-work to conquer depression. Rarely can it be done alone. Isolation was a big problem for me, but now I am more outgoing. I've developed an ability to connect with people. The cloak of depression that was hiding me has been lifted, allowing the real me to emerge.

To me, the least important criticism of antidepressants is their effect on sex. Chasing the big "O" can be frustrating for anyone. The temptation to get bored and to give up can happen to anyone, regardless of what medication is involved. The trick is to be creative and try something new. Which is, of course, the whole point. Change is life.

Gloria Valenti lives in New Jersey.

At the end of November 1993, I began to feel deeply depressed. I had just finished leading a ten-week study group based on "Healing and the Mind with Bill Moyers," a five-part television program on alternative medicine and mind–body healing. The day after the study group ended, I came down with a serious cold, a kind of flu, that lasted until the end of December, possibly into January. I took to bed, and that was the beginning of descent; my energy just all went inward.

I kept sinking lower and lower. It became difficult for me to get out of bed in the morning. There was just nothing I wanted to do. I had absolutely no motivation, even to do the least little thing was an incredible chore. And then with the weather that winter, which was so horrible with all the snow and the ice and the nonstop storming, I rarely went out of the house.

I went on like this for a while until I got scared. When I really panicked, I would look up names of practitioners, therapists in the area, and I would make a phone call. Sometimes I would even go see one. I found a transpersonal therapist who also does therapeutic touch, a form of energy-based bodywork. I had taken a meditation workshop with her. I knew a little bit about her, and I knew that she had been through her own healing process.

After several sessions with this therapist, she said to me that she felt I should check into antidepressant medication.

She didn't push it; she said it was entirely up to me. It was interesting to me that she would suggest medication, because she is really based in the holistic realm of health care and is a proponent of mind–body healing and spiritual integration.

I'd had experience twelve years ago with taking various psychotropic medications. I liked to feel I was beyond medication. So there was a little bit of pride, maybe, in not wanting to go on an antidepressant.

In February 1994 I enrolled in a transpersonal body–mind healing arts training program, so that I could get myself doing some activity. I felt kind of silly—phony in a way, or maybe like a failure—learning to do body–mind healing while at the same time thinking of taking a traditional, conventional chemical to alleviate my own problems. As time went on, I realized I did need something to break the downward spiral I was in. I had tried herbs, aromatherapy, and homeopathy on my own. I got some results but couldn't sustain the effort; it had become a chemical imbalance in my body or my brain. I just didn't have whatever it would have taken, whether it was willpower, motivation, or physical energy.

My therapist talked to me about the importance of integrating the medical with the body–mind field. She said it isn't a good idea to discount what the medical field has to offer. She said it is important not to judge things, but to use what works for you.

I did some reading on the new antidepressants and talked it over with my boyfriend. I decided to go ahead with it, even though I was frightened about it. I went to a conventional psychiatrist for the medical evaluation and to get the prescription. He started me on 25 mg. of Zoloft a day for a week or two.

I was really nervous about it so I was very careful to make sure that I had a good, substantial meal every time I took it, to avoid nausea or severe headaches. Also, I used affirmations every time I took the medication. I did some deep breathing, and I repeated an affirmation about the effects that I was hoping for from the medication, the improvements I wanted to make in my life.

I have to say that I felt the effects right away. I felt increased energy, and I just felt lighter. The side effects that I had were some insomnia and feelings of agitation. I didn't have much in terms of the headaches or nausea. There were times when I felt very agitated, especially right after the dose was increased.

For more than a year I had been seeing a polarity practitioner, who does a form of energy-balancing bodywork and mind–body healing. At that point I was seeing her just about every week. She was a little skeptical about me taking the medication, because she was more into the natural healing methods. But she noticed a change in the energy in my body in a polarity session I had with her a day or two after I started Zoloft. I sensed it, too—I felt energy physically moving through my body as she worked with me.

In April 1994, I started with 25 mg. for one week, then went up to 50 mg. for a couple of weeks, 75 mg., and finally up to 100 mg., the dosage I'm currently taking. Every time the dose was increased, I'd get a strong boost for a few days. I'd start worrying because I thought I was feeling too happy or too good. There were some times when I'd think maybe I shouldn't be taking Zoloft, because it was a little scary.

My boyfriend noticed right away that I seemed much lighter and was easier to be around. Things weren't as hard for me to do, things like washing the dishes, which had been a monumental task in the past. I feel that Zoloft has made an incredible difference in my life.

Now I'm able to get up in the morning without any problem. My mood is pretty good. I don't feel a dread of the day the way I used to, or anxiety from not having plans, nor do I feel totally lost, as I did. I'm able to focus more on practical matters that I couldn't deal with too well before. This is contributing to harmony in my home and in my relationship.

I really learned a lot from integrating Zoloft with other kinds of remedies and practices. I'm continuing to pay attention to my diet, to get bodywork, and to go to my therapy sessions. Now in therapy, instead of digging out of the hole of depression, I'm working on setting goals for starting a private practice in energy-based healing, working on getting myself more out there in the world, doing things, making contributions.

One notable change I experienced was that I began to feel more trusting, or let's say less suspicious, of others, and less threatened. During my depression I felt perhaps somewhat ashamed. If someone asked me how I was, I didn't know what to say. I felt hopeless, helpless, and despairing. Once I took Zoloft and started to come out of the depression and to feel more energy, I felt less dependent, less vulnerable. So, therefore, I started to feel more open.

I was able to relate to others much better, especially to my boyfriend. Instead of expecting him to fill my needs, and being upset if he couldn't talk to me when I wanted to talk, I was more sensitive to him. I saw him more as a separate person with his own individual needs and problems. It has made our relationship easier, better, and so much more pleasant.

I remember one day when we went to a bookstore. I love books, and I love going to bookstores. A lot of times when I used to go into a bookstore, especially if it was a big bookstore with a good selection of interesting things, I would become overwhelmed. I'd start to get a panic attack. It's as though my interest in the books was bigger than me, as though all those books and all those interesting topics were more important than I was as an individual, as a person, as a being. I'd get so overwhelmed with it—like I was a little child in a place of over-stimulation, without an adult there to protect her, or shield her, or give her limitations.

There was something about that day that made me feel really present. I was tuned in to my boyfriend and to the environment, not just to myself. It was a wonderful, peaceful, very, very happy feeling. I thought some miracle was happening. Of course it was just that day, and it didn't continue. But it was the beginning. Later on, I was able to return to that experience in a more gradual, paced way so that I grew with it and it developed in me. Now that way of behaving is a part of me, it's not just something that's happening to me.

I really felt like I was there, and the books were not bigger than me. My power as an individual, as a human being, was present. I was looking at them at my leisure; I didn't feel a sense of pressure or urgency that I must have these books or I must know all this information. It was just a totally and purely enjoyable experience. I attribute it to taking the medication.

Being on the medication, having more energy, and being in better spirits has helped me to continue doing the personal work that I needed to do, asserting myself in places where I needed to, continuing to grow in awareness or exercise awareness in my life.

I've been on the medication now for about four months. At six to eight months I'm hoping to come off of it, and perhaps switch to a more natural approach—various herbal treatments that can be used to maintain a good mood and health in general. But if that doesn't work for me, then I will gladly stay on the medication for as long as I need it. If that's for the rest of my life, then so be it.

Mary L. Miller, thirty-three, lives in Nevada. She is interested in researching family genealogy.

When I was nine years old, I told my mother I thought I needed a psychiatrist. I felt I was different from other people. My mother told me not to worry, I was just going through a phase. As I got older, I kept wondering when I was going to outgrow it.

What a relief to have my problem identified, after a lifetime, to have it named! It has a medical diagnosis, and best of all, a medical treatment. I can begin to learn what "normal" is like.

I have been taking Zoloft since March 1994, roughly six months, at the time of this writing. Before Zoloft, my life was completely out of control. I was fearful of everything and everybody. I wanted nothing to do with people, yet I craved human contact and acceptance. I was, however, functional. I held down a well-paying, rather stressful job in the insurance industry and was good at it. My bills were paid, my credit rating intact. Personal hygiene and grooming were excellent. Family life was comfortable. Despite all of this, I felt like a misfit, as though I were living in a world created for other people. Often I told those close to me that maybe I didn't belong on this planet. From time to time, I sought help but was steered toward cognitive therapists who told me nothing I didn't already know.

In March, I had a crying jag that would not pass. I'd been unemployed for eight months and was terrified about the future. I didn't want to live. I called a suicide hotline and got nowhere. In desperation, I called my primary doctor and begged for a referral through the HMO. The HMO referred me to a female psychiatrist, and the rest is history.

At first I experienced a little G.I. disturbance until my body got used to the medicine. I started with a quarter of a 50 mg. pill, using a pill cutter. Eventually I worked my way up to the present dosage, 150 mg. I have experienced no ill effects, even while taking both over-the-counter and prescription sinus medications needed for my recurrent sinus problems.

Zoloft has freed me from instability. For the first time in my conscious memory, I'm not at the mercy of my own mood swings. Morning traffic doesn't tense me up for the whole day. I listen better to customers and no longer perceive their problems as a direct result of my own inadequacy. There is no edge to my voice, thus, better communication and minimal confrontation.

Another big difference Zoloft has made in my life is in my perception of reality. Before, I was an emotional child locked in an adult body. My feelings, as reactions to various stimuli, were those of a child; I didn't get angry—instead, my feelings got hurt. The adult took a backseat and functioned primarily intellectually, knowing it was inappropriate to manifest the child's rage. I was constantly clashing with myself.

Zoloft has soothed the angry child so that the adult can grow. Now I'm learning how adults feel inside. Sometimes I amaze myself with how gracefully and maturely I handle different situations. Who is this articulate grown-up who lives within me? Is she really real, or medically induced? If I go off the medication, will she still be there or will I be like Cinderella at midnight? I'm afraid to find out, so I've never missed a dose.

I am grateful to have finally found the right therapist and the right treatment. I am sharing my experience in the hopes that it may help someone else. I am using my real name. I am not ashamed of what I am doing. I have a problem and I'm doing something about it.

Selina is a twenty-three-year-old living in Baltimore and working as a graphic designer. She enjoys cultivating the artist in herself, trying new and adventurous things.

When I was in high school, my mother and father's fights became more frequent, and living in my house was tense. I didn't know if they were headed for divorce. The only thing I did know was my mother was going through an extreme crisis of depression, for which she courageously hospitalized herself.

I graduated from high school and carried my anxieties and fears to college, where I studied graphic design at an art school in Baltimore, Maryland. I realized I loved creating art, even though I knew it was quite a subjective and critical field. I was enthusiastic but scared as hell.

By the time my sophomore year rolled around, the panic attacks about my schoolwork were getting worse and more frequent. Now the work was much more intense and demanding. I stressed out on every project and I cried an awful lot, almost every other day. I was so fearful of making a mistake that I often did not complete a project; I was paralyzed with panic and fear.

I started dating in my freshman year, and I made many friends. However, looking back, I see that I was very dependent on my boyfriend and close friends for almost everything. I had many inhibitions and couldn't let myself go or even want to get "it" over with. But I wasn't afraid to touch myself; I was more afraid to be sexual with another person. I was also self-conscious about my body, my hips and my face especially. I didn't feel like a woman; I still felt like an adolescent. Basically everything else—such as housecleaning, personal care, weight, finances—I actually managed all right.

I was sick with an upset stomach and irritated bowel syndrome more than once during the start of sophomore year. When I broke down to the doctor in the college health center, he gave me the name and number of a local social worker, who soon suggested I see a psychiatrist to discuss my alternatives with pharmacotherapy, in addition to psychotherapy to help my coping abilities with anxiety/panic and depression.

I was started on Pamelor [generic name: nortriptyline; tricyclic antidepressant], but within five weeks I knew my body wasn't liking this medicine. My doctor switched me to Prozac. I took one 20 mg. capsule every day for two years and five months. I had dry mouth and stomach upset, but I showed signs of improvement.

After six months on Prozac, I had lost ten pounds (I went down to ninety-two pounds) and I had trouble sleeping at night. My physician prescribed a low dosage of Sinequan [generic name: doxepin; tricyclic antidepressant] to help out with the sleeping and weight loss. In addition, I ate carbohydrates and drank nutritional supplements high in calories. All these things together did the trick. I still had a lot of anxiety, so my psychiatrist supervised me on BuSpar [generic name: buspirone; antianxiety drug] for about a year. I was responding so well to the BuSpar, my psychiatrist start weaning me off the Prozac, prescribing 20 mg. every other day, then putting more time between doses. But I had a relapse of depression and quickly went back to daily doses.

Many important things happened to me in 1993 that affected my therapy. Both my psychiatrist and my social worker moved, and I graduated from college. I learned to cope with life outside school and with new helpers. Since I was stopping the BuSpar (my anxiety was lessening) and I could not tolerate less or more of the Prozac, my new psychiatrist suggested that I try a new drug on the market called Paxil. It worked for three months with no major side effect except anorgasmia, which was quite frustrating!

So she and I decided to try yet another drug, Zoloft, which I still take today. The only thing I've experienced on this drug is nausea. I have found that I must be careful when taking medications such as antihistamines. I feel jittery and tired. Also, I think taking Zoloft on a full stomach helps to ease my digestion a bit.

My psychiatrist had me increasing the dosage much too fast for me, so I took the liberty of increasing it slowly. (I am currently up to 40 mg. a day.) I am the one in control of what I put in my body. What I find most important in drug therapy is careful supervision by the psychiatrist. A doctor needs to be considerate toward my body, and inform me of the nature and side effects of a particular drug.

I started seeing a new social worker soon after starting Zoloft. She and I proved to be an excellent match. To this day I am amazed at the progress I have made in a year. I am working at a small graphics firm, doing what I was taught in school. I have a healthy relationship with a young man with whom I share an apartment. I am more aware of my body and what goes into it. I see an acupuncturist to manage stress and anxiety and to build confidence. I may have a good cry every month or so, though I still panic! I am learning how to deal with panic and insecurities in therapy.

I would like to exercise, but I am not able to commit to it. What I am committed to is writing in a journal, writing stream-of-consciousness negative thoughts, turning negatives into positives, and other growth exercises. I have started wearing a rubber band on my wrist that I snap every time I think a negative thought. It's hard work to catch myself, but it helps with canceling negatives.

For about a year now, I have wanted to stop taking the Zoloft. I have problems coming to terms with the pros and cons of taking drugs. On the one hand, the Zoloft keeps me stable, and on the other, I don't like putting something man-made in my body. I want to have children someday, and it scares me to be on this drug when I could or want to get pregnant.

My personal goals have changed a lot over the years. I used to wonder, "Why am I still depressed? I should be over this already!" I have learned that I cannot get rid of anxiety or fear or depression. My goal has been to learn how to *manage* them. For me, it is important to feel needed, to feel productive, to feel creative, to feel free to create, work, and play without feeling guilty for things I have left undone or mistakes I have made in the past. I feel better as I accomplish some of these things every day, every week of my life. And if that means being on Zoloft for a couple more years, then so be it. Success does not come overnight in this struggle, but it will come if worked at.

Barbara N. lives in California.

Six years ago I was diagnosed with breast cancer. During the treatment and subsequent five-year waiting period, my anxiety about relapse was a prominent feature of my depression and, later, my hospitalization. Relapse is most likely to occur within the first five years after diagnosis.

I was first prescribed Prozac, along with Xanax to deal with jitteriness from the Prozac. Prozac made me too speedy and the headaches were horrendous. After being on Prozac a year, I was hospitalized; the two seem to me to be connected. There, I was taken off Prozac and put on a dose of at least 100 mg. (I can't remember the exact amount) of nortriptyline [brand names: Aventyl, Pamelor; tricyclic antidepressant], until my worsening urinary hesitancy caused my doctor to take me off. He scared me when he said it could be permanent.

Then I was prescribed Zoloft. In my first couple of days I had nausea but it went away. Sometimes it hasn't been enough. I've now been on a combination of medications for two years: 200 mg. of Zoloft, 15 mg. of BuSpar [generic name: buspirone; antianxiety drug], and 25 mg. of nortriptyline. BuSpar also has made a big difference in calming me down.

I'm not self-destructive anymore. I believe I'll need five years on a maximum dose of Zoloft to avoid relapse.

Nick Ellis is a musician, hospice worker, parent, and executive who lives in the Northwest. He has five great kids, health problems, and business successes and failures.

A type A personality, I have always been able to power up to handle very difficult challenges in my personal and professional life. I have been the president of two companies, the latest in such (hidden) financial shape that it was in undeclared bankruptcy.

In July 1993, I began to show clear signs of mental stress. I was agitated, easily distracted, showed loss of interest in my affairs, suffered from sleeplessness—I was really falling apart and I could not cover it up. I started psychiatric therapy in August, with an eye toward the "restoration of function."

By September my executive effectiveness had dropped by at least 50 percent. True, the business was in sorry shape. It became clear that I would not be able to power up enough energy and stamina to save the company.

I was diagnosed as mildly depressed since I seemed upbeat, extroverted, and full of physical energy, but as every week went on, my life became more difficult. Small problems became big ones, big ones became huge! I lost self-confidence. Therapy helped me understand where I was, that I needed to make a change in my life or I might lose it. But I insisted on staying on the job.

Enter Zoloft.

A good friend, who had worked as a consultant for me for the previous three years, cautiously recommended that I seek medication. No way, I said. She shared with me her Prozac story, telling me Prozac had enabled her to stop her downward depressive spiral.

I discussed the idea of medication with my therapist and with my primary physician. They started me on Zoloft, 25 mg. daily for a week, increasing it to 100 mg. after six weeks. I am a big man, 250 pounds. By the end of the third week, at 75 mg. daily, I felt the drug kick in.

The first thing I noticed was a significant reduction in fear and a restoration of self-confidence. I began to see problems in a prioritizable perspective. I was no longer overwhelmed, I felt no longer defeated. After two months, my up-and-down mood swings had flattened out, my physical and psychic energy restored to healthy levels.

At first I had no negative side effects. All who knew me could see the positive change in my personality and my capacity to lead. I was my old self, yet I did not have the constant restlessness that had belied my previously "happy" personality. I was aware of painful past experiences and potential threats to the future, but I was no longer pulled down by the past or fearful and threatened by the future.

I had been on Zoloft for five months when my boss killed himself. The owner was a young entrepreneur, obsessive-compulsive, who denied reality in his personal, business, and public affairs. At age thirty-seven, with a wife and three children, he killed himself. The truth is, while I am sorry for his children, he was toxic, berating, and abusive to people who worked for him. I was able to rise to the occasion and keep the company together. The widow and trustees put such pressure on me to perform, I decided to quit on my fifty-fourth birthday, a great present for myself, my family, and friends.

Sometime afterward, I experienced some sexual dysfunction, a first for me, of delayed or nonexistent ejaculation response. I consulted with my physician and a urologist. As I tapered down my Zoloft to zero, over a month, my ejaculation response returned to normal.

I have had a considerable reversal in my psychosocial being. I do not miss the Zoloft, but I truly doubt whether I would be where I am today without having had both psychotherapy and medication. Not only did the Zoloft allow me to pull myself out of the pits, it also made me aware that I had been in a depressive state for a long time. I am much more attuned to my body and mind. I am more centered, far less restless. I face the rest of my life with a more calm and inner-directed nature.

Zoloft worked.

Jennifer Green Woodhull is a journalist and freelance writer. She walks her dog, Egg, on the plains of Colorado.

I am a committed Buddhist of ten years' standing. Every day I swallow 125 mg. of Zoloft. It wasn't an easy decision. And it has changed my life.

Meditation and medication went to war in my mind when I moved from easygoing Boulder, Colorado, to Juneau, Alaska. Neither the climate nor the social milieu agreed with me. For the first time in my life, I couldn't find work or friends. I turned to the clear light of the Buddhist teachings, only to find it eclipsed by my despair.

I began entertaining serious doubts about Buddhism. Experiences that had once stimulated my curiosity, like doubt and critical contemplation, assumed ominous overtones. I felt the shame of a heretic, painfully coupled with the defiance of a reformer.

Frightened, and plagued by a chronic, stress-related shortness of breath, I asked a psychiatrist for Valium. She shocked me by suggesting antidepressants instead. An occasional pill for acute symptoms was one thing, but daily, mood-altering biochemicals? My spiritual practice required an uncontaminated mind. Cursing the doctor's arrogance and ignorance, I rejected her pills and intensified my meditation practice.

Things got worse. My long-suffering partner supported me as best she could, but we no longer shared the same reality. My world was relentlessly grim and cruel. Even TV nature specials, my one reliable dose of color amidst Juneau's gray mists, horrified me with images of lustful bull seals mindlessly crushing their mates and pups. I'd finally landed a job, but my experience as a news reporter only deepened a bitter conviction that rich, white men were consistently brutalizing and robbing everyone else.

Of course, these perceptions aren't entirely delusional. But the challenge, for a Buddhist, is to work with what you perceive. I seemed to be lacking the proper tools for the job. My spiritual beliefs were no help.

Suicide, I knew, would only intensify and prolong my karma. I feared the weight of existence would crush my heart, leaving me, like some ghoul in an Edgar Allan Poe story, to stumble in agony through infinite lifetimes.

After two years of severe depression, I returned to the Rocky Mountains for three months of intensive Buddhist practice and study. I attended classes, meditated, and resolved to leave my misery behind in Juneau. But not even Colorado's famous sunshine could break the thrall.

By the end of my retreat, Buddhism had become just another instrument of torture. I must be terribly flawed, I reasoned, to come away starving from such a lavish spiritual feast. My options presented themselves in black and white. Giving in to the lure of a chemical fix meant giving up my faith in Buddhist practice as the ultimate remedy for suffering. Besides, wasn't this pain my karmic kismet? Popping pills would only postpone, even compound, the inescapable effects of my own actions.

Desperate, I consulted a therapist. She explained that years of fearful, negative thinking had, figuratively speaking, worn a groove in my brain. The SSRIs seem to help thoughts jump that groove, paving the way for new patterns of perception. "They may be very helpful for you," she ventured. My body relaxed. I explored my family tree and found depressives scattered liberally through three generations. It struck me that isolation and anxiety had haunted me since childhood. The shock of living in Juneau, sans friends, job, or sunshine, had burst open a trunk jam-packed with lifelong anguish.

But none of these revelations relieved my spiritual conflict until I realized suddenly—while meditating, as it happens—that I'd already decided to take antidepressants. I'd made that decision at the moment my therapist gave form to the possibility. My conflict wasn't about making that choice, but about whether my decision made me a good or bad person.

The clouds began to dissipate. On the question of fundamental morality, Buddhism is unflinchingly clear. Basic goodness is a birthright that exists beyond conventional concepts of good and bad. My distorted logic had blinded me to my own incorruptible nature. It followed, then, that using medication wasn't a rejection of my path. It was part of it.

In this context, to fail to trust my decision amounted to a form of hubris. It occurred to me that by joining the legions of SSRI users, I'd gain the informed compassion born of shared experience, so highly valued by Buddhists.

I sought out another psychiatrist. She prescribed Zoloft.

My life has changed in ways both subtle and profound. Joy doesn't suffuse me, but it's available again. Bad days are no longer debilitating. Most important, my anguish doesn't fill the screen. Before Zoloft, the self-absorption of extreme suffering had blotted out virtually all curiosity and compassion. I still suffer, of course; that's the human condition. But the pain of existence no longer absorbs my attention. I'm a great deal more taken with the Canada geese loudly littering the autumn sky.

These days, I distinguish between the brain and the spiritual entity that is mind. That distinction makes medicating a malfunctioning brain no more profane than the use of digitalis for afflictions of the heart.

Still, I ask myself what surprises await me down the line. I worry that my miracle drug, like everything else, travels with its own shadow. I simply haven't danced with Zoloft long enough to learn how the shadow moves. For me, the risk is worth it.

All I ask of my little yellow pills is that they buy me time while I reconfigure my interpretation of the world. If I craved euphoria, I'd look for other drugs. What I want is the capacity to see things as they are: neither sacred nor profane; neither ripe with mystical significance nor tragically drained of meaning.

Recently a concerned Buddhist student questioned his teacher about the growing use of antidepressants. "In Tibet," the teacher answered, "we have a saying. When you are sick, pray for medication. But pray not to take the medication too long."

Somebody say amen.

Maria C. is a thirty-year-old woman living on the central coast of California, with plans to return to college, travel to Europe, spend time with her sisters, and enjoy life to the fullest.

The very first medication—I don't know its name—given to me for a psychiatric condition was when I was seven or eight. I remember a neighbor, who was a physician, coming over to give me injections while I was held down, to calm my violent, horrendous temper tantrums. He was a big man, he carried a bag, and what he did hurt.

My father died young of renal failure. I'm the youngest of a large family, five girls and one boy. My mother's drinking was getting progressively worse by the time I was in high school. By then, everyone was out of the house except my mother and me. I never knew what to expect when I'd come in the front door.

With a therapist's urging, I went to college in Florida, leaving behind a longtime boyfriend and my mother. My mother was dying of cirrhosis back in Connecticut but I had no idea how quickly. I came home for Christmas vacation on December 20, 1983, went directly into the arms of my boyfriend, contacted friends also home on vacation, and went to see my mother in the hospital on the twenty-second.

"It's Maria, Mom." She said my name. I'll never know if she just mimicked me or if she knew me. I left the hospital for the night. I wish I had stayed, God, I wish I'd stayed. I was in bed with my boyfriend at 2:00 A.M. when my sister swung the door open and said, "Mom's died. We're going to see her. Get dressed."

I went back to school, played on the beach, drank away misery, guilt, and self-loathing. Long periods of despair and hopelessness alternated with spells of confidence, energy, and elation. Shortly thereafter, with my boyfriend and inheritances in hand, I went to Denver. My boyfriend landed a job he was successful in; I dabbled in waitressing and had friends.

I went on a one-month trip to Mexico and Central America that lasted three and a half years. In Mexico I met a man, a nightclub owner. I became caught up in a wild European community in the very south of Mexico, where a tropical, lush port looked like—and can be—a paradise. Running around beaches topless, drinking margaritas and Coronas, taking trips to other exotic locations, buying whatever my heart desired, having servants and a man who adored me: this seemed to be it. I fell right out of contact with my family and friends, meanwhile promising my boyfriend in the States I'd be home "next week," "next week."

I had the best and worst times of my life there. Three and a half years of alcohol abuse finally brought my health to very near a fatal bottom. Hepatitis, repeated flus, long-term diarrhea, extreme weight fluctuation, crying jags, and guilt for not being the typical Connecticut professional drove everything else in my life to excess. In 1991 a nasty fight with my lover had me drunkenly on a plane to the States.

I showed up at my sister's in San Francisco a physical and emotional disaster. I cried all the time. Staying with my sister didn't work, so I relocated a couple of hours south. Depression hit hard. Gone was the vibrant, gregarious Maria. I felt as if I had a bag over my head or a thick, hazy fog suffocating me, which no matter where I went was with me. My vision was distorted, as if I were looking at the world through a pair of dark glasses with the wrong prescription. A once avid reader, I could no longer concentrate and the words jumped off the page and around in my head. Once enjoyable and soothing, music was pain, throwing me into crying jags. Eating—who cared? Certainly not me.

A few weeks later, I slit my left wrist. Thus began the frenetic roller-coaster ride that I have only recently stepped off. I was repeatedly certified as a danger to myself—according to state law, they can hold you in fourteen-day increments. I was diagnosed manic-depressive.

I was given Prozac, to no effect. I didn't feel any different. I was given Haldol [generic name: haloperidol; antipsychotic drug]. I don't know why. Though I had trouble with many thoughts colliding and crashing in my head, Haldol blurred my vision and made me sluggish. They gave me lithium [brand names: Lithane, Carbolith; mood stabilizer], which blew me up like a balloon, thirty pounds in all. I was water everywhere; my face seemed thick, my ankles invisible, and my body heavy. Of course this added to the depression, for I always took pride in my appearance. I was switched to Mellaril [generic name: thioridazine; antipsychotic drug]. I felt heavily drugged, less in touch with the intensity of my depression, more numb. I took and tried everything they suggested.

I always have had bad sleeping problems, having to use a light or TV to get to sleep. Klonopin [generic name: clonazepam; antianxiety drug], coupled with the other medications, seemed finally to allow me to sleep. Out of the hospital for a time, I rejoined AA—I had attended meetings upon my return from Mexico—and began to work with a sponsor, but depression loomed.

Elavil [generic name: amitriptyline; tricyclic antidepressant], Desyrel [generic name: trazodone; serotonin agonist], Stelazine [generic name: trifluoperazine; antipsychotic drug], Thorazine [generic name: chlorpromazine; antipsychotic drug], Valium [generic name: diazepam; antianxiety drug], Paxil, and imipramine [brand names: Tofranil, Janimine; tricyclic antidepressant] followed in the next two and a half years of hospitalizations. None of them did a thing, and frustration turned into even deeper hopelessness. My depression plummeted to unimaginable depths. No medication would ever help, and no psychiatrist could treat or fix this. Didn't they know fate had doomed me? I was a lost cause, let it rest. They shoot wounded horses, don't they?

I felt as if I were slipping deeper and deeper—more attempted suicides, hospitalizations, anorexia, running AWOL from the hospital, hypomania, and violence—before I ended up in a new hospital with a new set of doctors. I was given Zoloft, in addition to my other medications. One month later I left the hospital. I cried the whole way home, but I didn't think of jumping out of the car. Soon I thought maybe I could get something resembling a life. I had a bit more energy; I made a list of issues I thought should be worked on with my therapist; I called my AA sponsor to ask if she would work with me again; I began buying tapes for my Jeep and put in a new stereo system; I pulled out clothing I used to wear; and I got a new library card.

If I hadn't had all those legal holds keeping me hospitalized, I doubt I'd be writing this now. I want to reach through this book and grab the family member, the friend, and especially the suffering person reading this to say eye-to-eye that it can and does get better. Time, patience, and a lot of trial and error go into finding an antidepressant that works. Zoloft did it for me, not immediately, and the change was subtle when it began to take effect.

Now I treasure spending time with friends and housemates, sharing womanly feelings and ideas about men and sex, careers and dreams. Instead of worrying about the most painless method of suicide, I worry about how I can cram all I want to do into a day. The bottom line is that I'm back, and according to family and friends, I am better than ever. It's when you struggle through something like this that you can let out a sigh of relief and say, "Boy, that was painful, really shitty, but worth it because look at what I've learned and look at all there is left to learn, from one another but especially from myself."

Maybe one day I won't need antidepressants; maybe I always will. That's not important. Today is important and today I took my Zoloft, did some AA work, ran a few errands, and am now lying in the sun with my best friend next to me. Today is beautiful! I'm growing spiritually and I'm growing intellectually, and I have faith I will strike a balance in both areas. And last night I turned off the light and the TV, and I went to sleep in silence.

May S. Solomon lives with her husband and children in Virginia.

I've been depressed since I was a young teen. At the age of fourteen, I impulsively tried to kill myself by overdosing on a prescribed allergy medication. I cried so hard when taking the pills that I couldn't swallow many of them. This attempt was not a call for help. I never revealed it to anyone until many years later—not even my best friend. At age fifteen, I planned how I would kill myself at seventeen. At seventeen, I extended the time until nineteen, to see if I might be happier with life then. I felt like a misfit, misunderstood, and dumb. I was overly sensitive, shy, and awkward.

I sought professional help when I was in college and have seen six additional therapists over the years (in individual, marital, or group counseling). Because I've always presented myself as a highly functioning woman, all therapists except the last missed seeing the depth of my pain, no matter what words I used. I forced myself to do well in everything because I did not want to live the constricted, isolated life my mother had as a result of her untreated anxiety and depression.

During the three years of treatment with my last therapist (which ended a year ago when I was forty-five), I worked on my widespread anxieties and depression. As my anxieties began to decrease, I became more aware of the layer of unhappiness beneath. I addressed childhood sexual abuse issues for the first time. I had always remembered a piece of the abuse, but had minimized it.

It was about two years into my therapy when I became depressed enough that my therapist recommended I consider antidepressants. I was crying a lot, had little energy, and was upset that therapy seemed unending. I totally rejected my therapist's recommendation for medication. I wasn't severely depressed—I would tough it out. After all, I always had. However, a year later, shortly before terminating therapy, I changed my mind and made an appointment with a psychiatrist for a medication evaluation.

Two factors influenced my decision. First, my therapist had disclosed that she was taking an antidepressant. Somehow that made it okay for me to be on one. After all, I also am a therapist by profession, so the stigma of a therapist taking an antidepressant was lessened. Yet that alone wasn't enough to sway me, and neither were the positive experiences that a good number of my clients were having on antidepressants.

The second factor involved a visit to a rheumatologist for an evaluation of pain over many parts of my body—most of which I had had for years. The doctor told me my symptoms were somewhat consistent with fibromyalgia, which he found responsive to antidepressants, but that my personality wasn't typical of a fibromyalgia patient. Nonetheless, I decided to take the plunge.

My husband was totally nonsupportive of my decision. All he could relate to was his uncle, who had been marginally responsive to antidepressants and had undergone shock treatment. He thought if I took antidepressants I would become a zombie like his uncle. He couldn't even begin to see how antidepressants might help. Luckily, I knew enough about the different kinds of antidepressants and the various ways people respond to them to not be too put off by my husband's remarks.

I began taking a low dose (25 mg.) of Zoloft, since my body is highly sensitive to medications. By my fourth dose, I awoke the following morning feeling far less groggy than usual and less "down." The world visually looked different. Everything looked sharper, brighter and deeper in color, much as if the sharpness, contrast, and color level on a TV had been raised. Sounds became clearer. I had the sense I was hearing more fully, taking more in. I also was unusually thirsty (and happy about it since I knew I never drank enough fluids for my own good).

One week after the effects of Zoloft had kicked in, I tried to search for the down feeling inside. I could call it up, but was unable to sustain it for more than a few seconds. It was truly incredible! I then increased my medication to a full dose (50 mg.). A few days later I began to feel something like a mild electrical current buzzing through my body, something akin to feeling jittery. Then I began to have trouble falling asleep. That had never been a problem for me before. I had always enjoyed sleeping, requiring nine and a half hours to feel fully rested. My psychiatrist reduced my dosage to 25 mg. The symptoms began to alleviate and I found myself only needing eight hours of sleep.

After one month on Zoloft, I had more energy than I had had in twenty-five or thirty years. When I awoke each morning, after fifteen or twenty minutes I felt as if it were midafternoon, when I typically would feel my energy building. Prior to Zoloft I kept a magnet on the refrigerator that read I Don't Do Mornings. It was no longer needed! I also began to have an appetite in the morning, which I hadn't had since my teens. Best of all, and least expected, I began to experience anxiety differently. It had always affected my stomach, which would feel tingly and do flips. Now, even upon parasailing for the first time, my stomach didn't react. In fact, I didn't feel my stomach at all. I remember touching it just to make sure it was still there.

It dawned on me that I had not felt anxious during parasailing, only excited. I felt a distinct sense of loss, but it was surely something I could get used to! In circumstance after circumstance, my physical experience of anxiety was minimized or gone. For the first time in dozens of years I felt truly normal. My memory and ability to concentrate significantly improved. Although I had been a straight A student in graduate school, I had to work ridiculously hard to do well. Learning never came easy to me. I assumed I had an undiagnosed learning disability. Now I wonder if Zoloft has cured my learning disability, or whether my difficulty learning was a result of an underlying depression that had impacted my ability to concentrate and remember things.

Another change I experienced on Zoloft was a reduction in the number of intestinal upsets—down from once or twice a week to maybe twice a month. Although I never thought of myself as having PMS, I also found that any irritability prior to my period was gone, and that my breasts and stomach swelled less. More unexplained, for many years my nose, hands, and feet were usually cold to the touch, and I always wanted a room five or more degrees warmer than most. Now I seem to have a more normal body temperature, and my nose, hands, and feet are rarely cold. And when they are, it is uncomfortable but it doesn't "hurt" like it used to. The only negative effect I have noticed has been weight gain—fifteen pounds over the year. Since I'm five-feet-eight-inches and now weigh 160 pounds, it isn't terrible, and I know I will deal with it sometime soon. For now, I'm simply concentrating on enjoying all the positive aspects of being on Zoloft.

Life indeed is a thousand times better. I get along better with my husband, though he says he doesn't see any changes in me. Compared to what he had expected, I take that as a compliment! But I have noticed that my sex drive has increased. Aside from my husband's perceptions, my kids also say they see no change in me. I find that hard to believe since for me my whole life feels changed, but obviously the changes are within—where it really counts.

One thing I need to mention is that over the year that I've been on Zoloft, I have varied my dose. If I feel any PMS-type symptoms prior to my period, I increase my dosage by 25 mg. Also, if for any reason I begin to feel down for more than a day or two, I increase my dosage by 25 mg. and then reduce it when I feel better. Once, a couple of months into taking Zoloft, it just stopped working. I don't know why. I called my doctor, who told me I could play with the dosage as needed. The most I've ever taken is 125 mg. Generally, I take between 50 and 100 mg. I simply listen to my body and let it guide me. I am thankful that my doctor has trusted me enough to encourage me to adjust the dosage.

At this point on my journey with Zoloft, I wonder about four things. First, what my life would have been like if I had taken it back when I was a depressed teen. Second, what the long-term effects are—let's say, after twenty-five years. Third, I think about when I should begin to wean myself off of medication. A part of me is tempted to never try. Life is too good. Last, I sometimes wonder what our world would be like if antidepressants were in the water supply. Oh, for those who might react negatively to antidepressants, have no fear. In my fantasy, unadulterated water will still be available at your local grocery store.

Mary Smith lives in a suburb of Boston. She is fifty-six years old.

I'm a manic-depressive woman. Because I'm faithfully on lithium [brand name: Eskalith; mood stabilizer] (since 1979), I rarely have mood swings. I ended up adding Zoloft to my medications because I was depressed. My brother was on it and said it made a huge difference for him when he was climbing out of a crippling depression. I was working as a home health aide and gradually slipped into depression. I was insecure, anxious, and going to bed about six-thirty at night, totally exhausted. I hid it as best I could.

Luckily I had just joined an HMO and was referred to a psychiatrist. He increased my lithium and put me on a small dose of Zoloft.

Of course, nothing happened for two weeks. Then the lenses were lifted off my eyes, and I began to see my world again in a positive way. I was in an optimistic mode, feeling competent.

I had no side effects, except dry mouth and a total lack of sex drive—that was okay because I wasn't seeing my companion then.

Later I was upped to one and a half tablets; now I'm back to one. I don't know how long I'll be on Zoloft, but I'm not fearful. This was a temporary setback, and I'm fine now. Hurrah for SSRIs.

Dianne Nola is a part-time hair stylist, voice-over actress, and musician. She lives in California.

A day doesn't go by without my questioning whether my life would be easier, in certain ways, on medication. It's true, I don't have the calmness I used to have while taking Trilafon [generic name: perphenazine; anitpsychotic and antianxiety drug]. I have made the choice to stop taking medication.

I have always suffered from extreme mood swings. I believe they began in puberty. I have tried linking them to my menstrual cycle, the moon, diet, exercise, and external causes. I've charted and graphed. I've read many books and spoken with many people.

About four years ago, in the depths of one of my black periods, I checked myself into a psychiatric ward. I thought I was going crazy, I was certain I was bipolar and really didn't know what else to do. After many years of experiencing alternative healing methods, I gave up. I was exhausted with therapy and trying to heal myself in a "natural" way. I wanted a psychiatrist. I wanted help.

I was immediately placed on a low dosage of Trilafon. Along with that, I took Cogentin [generic name: benztropine; anticholinergic], which alleviates the spasms that can come as a side effect of the Trilafon. My sleeping time increased from seven or eight hours a night to between eight and eleven hours. I always felt slightly drowsy. Over the course of the next several years, we tried various dosages of Desyrel [generic name: trazodone; seratonin agonist], Prozac, and Zoloft.

Nothing seemed to affect my depressions. Finally, after two and a half years on medication, I hit one of my most severe depressions. They have always been extremely intense, yet relatively short. This one, however, lasted many months, with crying every day and seeing no reason to live—wishing an accident would just happen to take me anywhere but where I was at the moment. Negative voices spiraled everywhere around me. Again, I didn't know where to turn. None of the antidepressants seemed to work.

In desperation, I decided to speak with a psychic, referred to me by a close friend. Through that session I received a strong vision that I needed to find a therapist who integrated bodywork within psychotherapy. I shopped for about three months, absolutely determined to get what I needed. When I found Marie, my life slowly began to change. She was different from all the other therapists I had had in the past.

Every session felt like some kind of déjà vu experience. I feel that Marie is a soul sister for me. Besides having a master's in women's spirituality, she is well versed in Native American wisdom. We have worked a lot with visualizing and dreamwork, always incorporating the body. My first vivid breakthrough came in a dream. For months, all I had had were nightmares. Spliced in between them one night, I was ecstatically dancing. I have danced since I was about five years old. My theater arts major in college was essentially comprised of modern dance classes.

Yet, I realized I had stopped dancing. That's when I began again. Marie encouraged me to dance and explore my emotions through it. I was exposed to Gabrielle Roth's teachings, shamanic methods to be used in creative and performing arts, which furthered my search. Through the course of our session work, Marie witnessed my plunging deeply but unwillingly into different emotional states. I was angry that I had no control in these powerful whirlpools. I started learning how to accept them, and to realize that they do pass. At one point, I did quite a bit of research on psychiatric drugs. I was still on Zoloft and had no sexual appetite at all. I felt nothing. I also thought that there was too much of a risk for me to continue taking Trilafon.

What I really wanted was to go off all the medication, and I did just that. The process took about four months. God, it was strange. It was like returning to this person I used to know—me. I really got a sense of what the medication had done for me at that point.

I felt like thick, heavy blankets were being lifted off. I lost comfort but gained mobility. I felt alive. My energy was overwhelming. It still can be. Sometimes my mind feels like it's disconnected from my body and whirling in space. At those times, I SLOW DOWN. I have a daily practice of yoga. I exercise regularly. I have to be very aware of what I put in my body. It's very painful for me to be in any kind of disruptive environment. Some have likened it to a handicap, being as sensitive as I am. I truly believe I experience more beauty and pain than most people. I chose to go off of drugs. I think using psychiatric drugs can be a tool to ease oneself into another area for greater healing. Not using medication is a trade-off for me. For now, I choose to experience my *fire*.

Jeff Daniells lives in California.

All my life I was very shy. I really thought it was something that would never go away. Always very hard to meet people, and especially hard to speak in front of large groups. A few personality traits I did like were being very organized and responsible. An avid letter writer and pen pal.

The littlest things in life were naturally blown up to be big events. I worried a lot and was stressed out—always rushing around to straighten things up, organize things. Everything had its own place. I really got a lot done that way, but the stress was unbearable.

I went through most of my life like that, never thinking there was anything I could do about it. And from age fifteen to age thirty, I medicated myself with alcohol and drugs. That seemed to fill the gap. Allowed me to fit in and be more outgoing. But it was a roller coaster of a lifestyle, a large price to pay.

After I got clean and sober, and two or three years of therapy, my therapist recommended Zoloft. I didn't want to take any drugs. I was having a lot of trouble meeting people, a lot of trouble trying new things; having a lot of anxiety, even going into a place I'd never been, or even a new restaurant. Of course, it was better if I was with a friend. But alone, it was next to impossible. I'd feel nervous, clumsy, awkward, like everyone was looking at me and laughing to themselves. I'm five-feet-seven-inches, 150 pounds, and have been told I'm attractive, but never felt like it. Always short on self-esteem. I've worked in the restaurant business for more than fifteen years. And people are amazed that I do what I do, being so shy or "social-phobic." But it is more like being a robot. The lines are rehearsed, over and over again. I'm a waiter and bartender by trade.

I went through a period of loneliness and depression for about two months—insomnia during the night and sleeping out of boredom and depression during the day. I always managed to be responsible, going to work and doing what needed to be done. But I just wasn't happy. Felt like the color had gone out of my black-and-white life. A little melodramatic, I know, but that's how I felt. I'd given up on life, lost all hope.

When I went to a doctor about the depression, he recommended antidepressants. I told him my therapist had recommended Zoloft in the past. So, about five months ago, I started taking Zoloft. It took three or four weeks for me to see a difference. And then it was very subtle. The effects, in the beginning, were as follows:

1. Feeling of detachment. Like my body was driving a car but my mind was relaxed and sitting in the backseat. Couldn't maintain a train of thought, or listen to a conversation, for more than two minutes. This lasted two or three days.
2. Nausea, dry heaves even, at times. Lasted two days.
3. Constipation. Lasted about four weeks.
4. Weight loss of eight to ten pounds. Maintained weight loss for more than four and a half months.
5. Wired and tired at the same time. Lasted about one month.
6. I could get an erection, but it took forever. And sometimes impossible to reach an orgasm. Lasted one month.

7. My obsessive behavior and depression just gradually faded away, without me really even noticing, after about four to five weeks.

I was expecting more of a personality change, and a light feeling of being sedated. But I almost didn't think I was getting enough results for the $170 per bottle, which I pay for with cash or a credit card. But after giving it another few weeks, and talking to my therapist, I really compared the difference in my lifestyle before Zoloft and now. And now, I can see a nice change.

I expected to never have anything bother me, never get excited or stressed. I still feel all the normal feelings that everyone feels, but not to such a magnified degree. Not such drastic highs and lows. And I'm not so much in a hurry to organize the world—it's to a more normal level, and not so obsessive. If I get depressed, it lasts about two minutes, and fades away. I can calmly and constructively handle all of life's ups and downs. I can go into new places such as restaurants alone, still with a little anxiety, but a very small amount. An amount that I can get through. I'm not so spooked by people. I feel more that I fit in. Overall, I feel wonderful, and free. I feel that I have a new lease on life. Finally, I can enjoy life to its fullest and not be so constricted by anxiety and phobias.

After about four months, my doctor wanted to take me off Zoloft. He felt that the depression period had passed and I could function fine without the medication. But with all the other benefits I received, I really hated going off it. Plus, if I stopped and then started again later, I would have all the horrible side effects in the beginning. I'd rather stay on it. My therapist said that it would be better to leave me on it and let it be my choice when to go off it. That it was causing me too much anxiety thinking about stopping the medication when I wasn't ready.

I am very satisfied with Zoloft. I think it's wonderful. The only side effect I have is I clench my teeth or grind them. But that's sometimes, and when I catch myself, I stop it. Overall I think antidepressants are great. They allow people the freedom to be who and what they are, without being heavily medicated. I feel 100 percent normal. If I didn't see such a change in my personality, I wouldn't even know I'm taking anything.

Judith Duncan lives with her husband in Kansas City.

By the time I decided to start taking Zoloft in July 1992, I had come to the realization that I had been struggling with depression all my life. I was in my twenties before I entered therapy; however, I knew before then that something was wrong. As a teenager, I would fall into a depression that included long crying jags that would leave me sick and exhausted.

By the time I was thirty, I had seen four different therapists, but it wasn't until the fourth that medication was suggested. Even then, it wasn't to treat depression but chest pains associated with anxiety. At that time, I had a heavy workload and was experiencing marital problems. As my marriage disintegrated, my depression and anxiety increased to the point that my health deteriorated. However, no one felt that I needed any type of antidepressant, and I don't think that I would have taken one had it been recommended. I truly felt that I could "tough it out" and that if I began to take medication, I would never be able to stop.

My feelings changed after my divorce and subsequent second marriage. My husband and I moved to the southwestern United States. The move was a tremendous blow for me. This was the farthest that I had ever lived from my family, to whom I was very close. I left behind a lot of friends. I had a very difficult time finding a job because I wasn't bilingual. Consequently, I continually found fault with our new home. Although I eventually found a good job and made new friends, all I thought about or talked about was how much I hated where I lived. I hated to go shopping or even out of the house, because it meant going out into the city I despised so much. Finally, after a particularly disastrous Fourth of July weekend, my husband and I agreed that I needed help beyond just counseling—and that I needed to get it before our marriage became a casualty of my depression.

My therapist suggested Zoloft, after determining that I was suffering from obsessive-compulsive disorder (OCD). However, it was not clear what Zoloft would do to me beyond breaking the negative feedback loop that continually played in my head. It might make me hyper; it might not. It might reduce my libido; it might not. It might make me lose weight—or not. There were so many ifs that I wasn't sure what to expect. I only knew that I was ready to do anything to improve my outlook on life.

For starters, Zoloft made me hyper, all right. I experienced my first full-blown panic attack the first weekend I was taking it. Unfortunately, the attack came in the middle of the night during a visit with my parents. My mother, hearing me pace the floor, got up to find out what was wrong. I admitted to her that I was taking Zoloft. As she helped me, sweating and shaking, into bed, she told me that sometimes these drugs only magnify the symptoms they're supposed to alleviate. She held my hand and stroked my hair until I fell asleep.

I continued to take Zoloft for two years, and it *did* help me through a difficult period in my life. I was able to focus on my work. I quit obsessing over where I lived (although I didn't like it any better). I was able to fly, for the first time in my life, completely without fear. This was an accomplishment of major, major proportions! All good things, to be sure.

But for all Zoloft gave me, it exacted a price. I completely lost the urge to be creative or artistic—I had always kept some type of craft project going. My sex drive, which had been high, dropped to zero. Nothing affected me emotionally—I was neither very happy nor very sad about anything. I walked the emotional middle ground, reacting to events with the neutrality of a Stepford Wife. Consequently, because nothing affected me, I became more bold to say things that affected other people. I became more and more aggressive in my humor and in my criticism of others.

I also realized what a frightening dependence I had on Zoloft. If my schedule for taking it was disrupted, I would begin to feel a dull ache at the back of my head, accompanied by what felt like electrical shocks or buzzing. My thinking became sluggish. I would become very sleepy. People talking to me would seem very far away, as if I was under anesthesia. Sometimes, I couldn't function at all. I could only laugh, shrug my shoulders, and say, "I'm sorry. I can't help you."

When my husband and I moved again, I called a doctor in the new city and made an appointment to get another prescription for Zoloft. The appointment was six weeks away, and during that time, I made the decision to wean myself off the medication. I admit that I was scared. I wondered if the OCD would return. I suffered from headaches. I dreaded falling back into a depression. But when the day of the appointment arrived, I canceled it. I knew that I would rather be my own person than take a drug that somehow makes me less than what I am. And you know, even while I write this, I'm feeling a little down, but that's okay. Because that's the *real* me.

PAXIL

[generic name: paroxetine; selective serotonin reuptake inhibitor (SSRI); second-generation antidepressant with a shorter half-life than Prozac: 24 hours; therapeutic dose range: 10–60 mg. per day; FDA approved 1993]

Janis Atwood is from the Midwest.

I don't know if I willed it to happen or if genetic predisposition is really as powerful as my family professes it to be. My mother, sister, maternal grandparents, aunt, cousin, and, although I can't prove it, my father also, have experienced or are experiencing varying degrees of clinical depression. Most of these family members are or were at one time taking prescribed antidepressants. It's easy for me to think, then, that there is some biological, physiological thing going on here: I come from a long line of depressed people, which gives me good odds of being the same. On the other hand, because of all these depressed people around me, I think it could also be true that my environment could likewise affect me. Either way, depression is an undeniable reality of my life.

It has been eight months to the very day since I've had a beer. While this isn't particularly monumental in and of itself, it signifies something more important than the fact that I miss having a cold one with Mexican food or a good football game. In these eight beerless months, I have been medicated with Paxil. Paxil, I explain to the curious, is like Prozac's cousin without so many awful side effects. It's a little pink pill that I greet every morning with a swig of coffee. It's a thing that I love because it's made me like myself again, and also that I hate because I need it.

It's a complex little pill. For instance, I am to take it in the morning, yet the pharmacist has warned me with a bright yellow sticker on the bottle that it may cause drowsiness. Paxil has removed the overwhelming sadness that had blanketed my life, but it has also made me more emotionally neutral than anything else. It has regulated my sleeping but forces me to turn in much earlier than I'd prefer. But the question I've found most complex has been running in my mind for months: How will I know when I'm ready to stop taking it?

I do miss beer, as I've mentioned, and an occasional glass of wine I might have while eating dinner with friends. I've learned that my body doesn't do well with a mix of alcohol and antidepressant medication. Actually, the combination literally knocks me out. That is probably for the best, because it doesn't make much sense to ingest depressants (i.e., alcohol) when one is depressed anyway. Besides that, I have only experienced a few minor physical side effects with this medication. When I reach my apartment after three flights of steps, it feels like I have instead been spinning in a circle twenty times. And I definitely feel more drowsy since I've been on Paxil, which I think is easily explained by that "May Cause Drowsiness" sticker on the bottle. These side effects, I understand, are quite minimal. I'm one of the lucky ones.

Why did my "journey into Paxil" begin eight months ago? Perhaps it should have started earlier, but I didn't want to admit to myself, or to anyone else, that I might be truly depressed. Sure, I was down. But I could pull myself out of it, I hoped. My mother, a therapist and depression-sufferer, had urged me to take antidepressants for years—she is definitely of the genetic-predisposition philosophy. I almost took her advice several times. Yet I waited and waited until I was up against a wall.

Two years ago—two years after my sister survived a severe depression (thanks to medication and therapy)—I could no longer call myself feeling merely blue or down in the dumps. I was on the road to serious depression. I was still in college, my parents had recently divorced, a friend died in an accidental drowning. I didn't know what I wanted to do with myself or my life. I spent my last year of school wading in an existential crisis, paralyzed by fear of my future, tangled in a web of romantic relationships in which I was dishonest with myself and my partners. I struggled with my sexuality, my friendships, my family. Upon graduation, I took a job in a new city where I knew no one. I separated myself from my partner, my friends, all things familiar. I was a miserable workaholic who went home to watch hours and hours of television to which I paid no attention. I couldn't bring myself to think, to change, to feel anything but dread and sadness. Certainly, the things that were happening in my life were difficult, even depressing, but the weight of sadness I was carrying was far beyond my problems. Even when things in my life were going well, all I could feel was despair, guilt, helplessness.

I managed to go to a therapist, a wonderful woman who has helped me deal with my concrete problems. I came to accept therapy and Paxil as necessary healing parts of my life, perhaps temporary or perhaps permanent.

I am pleased with the steps I have taken to heal myself, but still I wonder: Was it circumstance that caused my depression? Or was it my fault? My genetics? Unhappy chemicals in my brain? My family? Still, I don't know. The question I am more concerned with, though, is when will I be ready to stop taking Paxil? Maybe I can't control the illness, but I am going to control my recovery. And I will recover.

Scott Riggs is a college student in Austin, Texas.

That I was put on an antidepressant came as a surprise to my family members, my friends, and myself. I lived a productive life and was outwardly very sociable and happy. My personal habits would suggest someone who was reasonably orderly (my room and my 1988 Toyota were kept clean, and I dressed reasonably well). I worked hard but still had fun. I'm a student at the University of Texas. I volunteered at AIDS Services of Austin as a buddy for someone living with AIDS. I had a lot to offer.

I had entered a drug trial for Pharmaco as a research volunteer. I was administered a hypoglycemic drug called glyburide and felt headaches not long after dosing. These headaches were like none I'd ever had. I got a feeling of empty-headedness, an inability to concentrate, and a diminished ability to sleep. Pharmaco was dismissive of my symptoms and displayed a very disturbing aloofness. It took a great deal of tact and diplomacy to bring them to agree to take responsibility for a visit to a neurologist. I had these headaches for a total of two months due to their reticence.

After the second week of these headaches, I did indeed become depressed. I couldn't fight an overwhelming sense of self-pity. I displayed the textbook signs of clinical depression, which I'd never had before. There have been reactive depressions in my life due to circumstances that I knew would be changed. This was quite different and I had no hope. I had my suicide planned were I to be deemed untreatable.

After a bit of exploration, the neurologist came up with an entirely physiological diagnosis: I'd become *hyper*glycemic. This was a springboard effect due to my personal habits. I was a marathon runner, running fifty miles a week, but I'd stopped a week before the study in order to follow the study protocol. This led to a "carb-loading" effect, since my three-thousand-calorie-a-day diet didn't change. The resultant epinephrine deficiency led to a serotonin deficiency from a "positive feedback loop."

The first night I took 10 mg. of Paxil at about six o'clock. I woke up at 3:00 A.M. with the most wonderful feeling I'd ever had: an appreciation of health. My symptoms—headaches, anxiety, facial flushing—were greatly diminished. I was healing.

It was two weeks into the semester and I was too far behind to catch up. I received a medical withdrawal. I had a little money in the bank and, for the first time in my life, I began to live. I worked, I bought a motorcycle, and I dated a woman who rolled her own cigarettes, drove a motorcycle, and had a tattoo. She was very much out of character for me. I was accustomed to dating librarianesque women. My sex life took off. Wait a minute. What was wrong with my sex life before? I had had a bad case of *ejaculatus rapidus*. On Paxil my sex life improved. For the first time, I had a hard time reaching orgasm.

On Paxil, I gained confidence while maintaining a sensitivity to others. I noticed how many subtle denigrations we dish on each other. I realized that the insecurities of others were placed on me and how readily I'd accepted this. With confidence came the ability to realize that my prior state was dysthymic; I had a chronic, low-level depression. The result was a redefinition of self while maintaining the core of myself. Although I felt totally different, to others I was merely more confident and outgoing. I was less inhibited. I realized that I have a lot to offer others.

My work performance blossomed. I became more effective on the job and was able to tactfully turn situations around that previously would have left me diminished and feeling irrelevant. I had a greater amount of energy and clarity of thought, as though a large portion of my brain was subconsciously devoting itself to solving problems I didn't know I had. All of this came at the moment that my headaches were gone. I don't have the words to describe how exalted I was to experience both simultaneously.

I was better on Paxil. What is meant by "better"? Where I had once seen new experiences as daunting, I now did not. I saw risk taking as worthwhile. I thought rewards in life that I'd long since dismissed as unobtainable or for other people were available to me. I now had a self-liking that made me open up to people as I never had before. I actively liked people and wanted to understand them better and know them more. I wanted to learn about myself through them. I was unafraid of closer contact and engagement. I began to understand that all of us have burdens and that these burdens shape us into who we are, while before I had felt like I was the only one who carried weight.

I saw myself open up to possibilities. A professor's recommendation that I go to med school was not ridiculous. I'd never set such high goals for myself. Depending on how well I do next semester, I may consider his suggestion. I can better fulfill my dreams with med school's high degree of training (I'd been preparing myself for nursing school). On Paxil, I also took on grandiose projects, projects that were unrealistic and fantastic. I toyed with possibilities that would have seemed absurd six months before. I considered trying acting, and like all second-rate actors, I fantasized about fame and fortune. Was I unrealistic to consider that I might have talents on the stage that only need further work and development? Don't all great actors pursue such dreams? Sure, but for every one of them that succeeds, there are thousands who fail. I'm reasonable enough to take it step by step. I'll take an acting class next semester.

I've made three efforts to stop taking Paxil. My facial flushing returned, along with a milder form of the headaches, on all three occasions. Things would go nicely unless there was a disruption in one of my romantic relationships. Then I would become dysfunctional.

I stopped running. It's almost like my running was a release that I no longer needed. Not surprisingly, during the recurrences of my headaches and symptoms of depression, I've felt the need to run. I've started smoking, which shocked everyone (including me). I've enjoyed new sensations and smoking is one of them. I'm sure I'll quit soon, but it's so much fun. Reckless? Probably. But I rationalize it by saying that I was merely inhibited before and now I'm more open to new experiences.

A spark came that led me to therapy. I'm new to this but am excited by the revelations that will come. I think that this may be Paxil's legacy. I'm hoping therapy will free me from Paxil by creating an emotional state similar to the drug's effects. I never would have been so interested in any of this if I'd never tasted how great life can be.

Kelli F. is in her early forties. She is a singer and musician.

I was always a very healthy, upbeat kind of person. When I turned thirty-nine, I started having a lot of physical problems and a great deal of stress. My kids were teenagers with the usual assortment of problems. I had been bulimic off and on since I was fourteen, but my bulimia now became very active. I was taking as many diet pills, caffeine pills, and laxatives as I could without being totally ill, and I was purging after almost every meal. I started having headaches, muscle and joint aches and pains, chronic sore throats, low-grade fever, and swollen glands. I was unable to concentrate or make decisions, and I was exhausted all the time.

I went to a family-practice physician who said I might have chronic fatigue immune dysfunction syndrome (CFIDS). He asked me a couple of times during the next two years if I was depressed or had crying spells for no reason. I didn't think I was depressed, and I told him I had good reasons for my crying spells. This doctor put me on amitriptyline [brand name: Elavil; tricyclic antidepressant], which is used as an immune system booster. I started on a low dosage and worked up slowly to the level he wanted. I only took it at bedtime, and it was very beneficial because it helped me to sleep.

In the next two years, I had kidney stones surgically removed, went through innumerable medical tests for every conceivable ailment, found out I had an ulcer and irritable bowel syndrome, and was still having tension headaches. It was at this time that my husband was offered a very good job in New Jersey, halfway across the United States from where we'd always lived in Iowa, and we moved.

We left an excellent doctor, our families, good friends, and a very active support system that I had greatly depended on during the last two difficult years. When we got to New Jersey, I just began to fall apart. It was a very stressful time. We lived in a hotel for a month with our three daughters; I couldn't find a job so I was doing temporary secretarial work; our house in Iowa didn't sell; and we had financial problems. I would get totally hysterical at times and scream and cry for hours at a time.

In December 1993, I began seeing a therapist. She sent me to a psychiatrist, because she thought I needed medication. The psychiatrist prescribed Paxil for the depression and Ativan [generic name: lorazepam; antianxiety drug] for my anxiety and the jitteriness that Paxil might cause. The psychiatrist said to play around with the two medications until I found a combination that worked. Both of them were started in small dosages and gradually worked up to a therapeutic level.

The psychiatrist gave me an information sheet on Paxil, but nothing on Ativan. Ativan is very addictive and I liked it right away. As soon as I took it, I was aware of being a great deal more relaxed and calm. It made my headaches better since it relieved stress. I had less anxiety and was somewhat groggy most of the time. I never felt jittery from the Paxil.

I did immediately begin suffering from constipation and a dry mouth, and soon noticed that I was unable to have an orgasm. I have always been able to have orgasms and attributed the problem now to the depression. Now I have been on Paxil for more than six months and still am unable to experience orgasms. I spoke to my psychiatrist about it eventually, and she gave me Periactin [generic name: cyproheptadine hydrochloride; antihistamine] to counteract the effects of the Paxil before I had sex. Periactin never worked for me, even though I tried taking it at different times and in different amounts for several weeks. I also took BuSpar [generic name: buspirone; antianxiety drug] for a while instead of Ativan, because it is nonaddictive. It didn't seem to do anything for me.

When I was dismissed from the psychiatric hospital I was in, I went to a day program where the psychiatrist tried me on Xanax [generic name: alprazolam; antianxiety drug] and later, Klonopin [generic name: clonazepam; antianxiety drug]. I wasn't told anything about them or their side effects except that they were addictive and I should take them only as prescribed. This psychiatrist also gradually reduced the Elavil until I wasn't taking it anymore.

I went into a different hospital at the end of February 1994. The doctor there lowered the level of Paxil I was taking because I was fainting periodically, and he thought it might be the Paxil. He also raised the level of Klonopin I was taking. This was very good for reducing my anxiety level, at which I've found Klonopin does a very good job, and I don't get the immediate-gratification feeling that I got from Ativan. He also started me on Desyrel [generic name: trazodone; serotonin agonist], which has a sedative effect, to help me sleep at night without panic and anxiety attacks in the morning.

I have been in and out of psychiatric hospitals now several more times. I am still depressed. I have cut myself several times. Self-injury is common among women who have been sexually abused as children. I have overdosed on pills two times, once on Klonopin and once on chlorpheniramine [brand names: Phenetron, Teldrin; antihistamine].

I am home now. I don't do much around the house and still have a great deal of difficulty concentrating and making decisions. I am still taking Paxil, Desyrel, and Klonopin. I can't have orgasms. I have wild mood swings from elation to despair in the same day, sometimes within the same hour. I am still seeing a therapist twice a week and my psychiatrist every two weeks. I gained weight when I was first depressed, about fifteen pounds, but I have lost all that and more. In fact, I am still slowly losing weight.

I am beginning to get back into some social activities, but being around people, especially strangers or crowds, is very difficult for me. Terry, my husband, is handling all the bills, all problems with our daughters, household chores, planning meals, almost everything. I try to help in small ways and be available to be supportive to both Terry and the girls, but it is difficult. Much of the time, I feel like my own problems and feelings are all I can handle and I just need to be away from everyone and everything. I still entertain thoughts of killing myself, but not too seriously anymore. So some things are better and some things are not. I am hopeful that with more therapy, I will soon be better and can go off the medications, especially Paxil.

Stephen Crossan lives in Virginia.

In 1984, after ten years at IBM, I learned that my creative-intuitive work style was different from the majority's deliberate, wise, and thoughtful approach to keeping things simple. I was unable to change my style to theirs in ninety days, even to save my job.

In 1986, I was surprised to find that the way I am is described in the *DSM-III* [*Diagnostic and Statistical Manual of Mental Disorders, Third Edition*] and given a name: manic-depressive illness or bipolar disorder. I could have lain low, as most of us do, to avoid an official diagnosis. Instead, I determined from the literature that there was no physical means of diagnosis other than behaviors during highs and lows. I read up on the "high" behaviors, practiced them, and signed up for medical disability as part of a manic but doomed plan to embarrass IBM into giving me my job back.

From 1986 to 1989, I worked for the Mental-Health Industry of Dane County, Wisconsin, as a full-time, professional consumer of mental-health services. My job, paid by SSDI [Social Security disability insurance], was to consume every service the professionals made available, help keep the waiting lists full, and somehow make it appear that all this was doing me some good. I joined "consumer" groups and attended conferences at the expense of various do-gooding organizations. I escaped from that life by the only means possible: an out-of-state job offer by an employer who didn't bother doing background checks.

Back in my birthplace of Arlington, Virginia, I lay low for three years and observed the odd behaviors of chronically stable people in their natural habitat: the U.S. Patent Office. While I found chronic stability to be a very serious and debilitating brain disease, sufferers were useful in that they tended to have good judgment most of the time—which we healthy bipolars often lack—and they were willing to do whatever mundane tasks they were assigned without thinking up new and innovative ways to do things differently. They could preserve stability and order while we bipolars suggested change and new ideas. We could cooperate and have progress, or clash and have mental illness. The question of who was ill was decided by majority vote: we bipolars lost.

When the chemical industry has a chemical imbalance problem in one of its processes, it tends to call on the services of a chemical engineer rather than a doctor. As a chemical engineer, and in consultation with the Lithium Information Center at the University of Wisconsin, Madison, and the Neuropsychiatric Institute of Copenhagen, I found a way in the spring of 1993 to abuse my lithium to maintain a state of stable hypomania while writing, doing my patent examiner job, and wheeling and dealing in real estate. The problem was that I had no lower safety net: In May–June 1993 the real estate deals went sour, I lost an important story contest, a ladyfriend lost interest in the marriage we'd been discussing. I lost interest in my job—refereeing as Xerox, Kodak, Canon, Dupont, etc., tried to patent every chemical and process that might someday be useful in copiers—and soon lost even the energy and ambition to get dressed to go to work.

I was not distressed by this turn of events. I saw it as a natural process by which bipolars without a needed contribution to make can lie low until something useful to do comes along. As a way of riding out the high-energy summer depression, I found I could induce a form of temporary brain death by marathon cable TV watching. The real estate opportunities I'd worked on became overwhelming worries, which I escaped by isolating myself in the new condo I'd been forced to buy and move into, and unplugging the phone. I refused to look at my mail, as the IRS seemed to be about to take legal action regarding past years' returns I'd been procrastinating over. I had plenty of food on hand—my manic spending sprees consist of buying all I can carry of whatever is half-price at a nearby Safeway—so I felt things were pretty much under control.

Unfortunately, my bosses and my father conspired to roust me from this low-energy existence and stick me in a for-maximum-profit psych hospital for "treatment." So it was that I was put on 20 mg. per day of Paxil, along with lithium two to three times a day. As this was a high-energy summer depression, raising serotonin levels could only make things worse, and did. On learning that I would be paying $500 per day after insurance to continue this miserable existence, I calmly went to lunch, had an extra Jell-O as a final farewell to the world, wrote a suicide note and holographic will, and made three suicide attempts in the bathroom of my room in the hour that my roommate was in group therapy. I knew better than to say anything about them to the staff, for fear of spending a week in four-point restraints.

Eventually, my father elevated my mood by getting my car inspected and helping me clear out a storage locker. The Paxil, of course, was credited. The doctor, on learning that my care was costing me real money, released me to a day program that cost me a third as much but still gave him $110 per five-minute daily consultation. On release, I took Paxil as ordered and had a fairly okay September.

Then, in October I crashed into my usual low-energy winter depression. Taking Paxil for months on and off made absolutely no difference in my moods, long-term or short-term. I got the impression that I was to keep taking it until my depression turned around on its own. Then the Paxil could be credited.

I ended up isolated in my condo again and was illegally fired for goldbricking just as the National Institutes of Health lured me out to Bethesda with the promise of $375 for a morning of PET scanning on and off the experimental antidepressant Idazoxan. The scans showed such classic bipolar depression that they offered me a four-month program of pink mystery pills. The only active ingredient turned out to be Idazoxan given at 40 mg. per day to fire me out of the winter depression (which may have been ready to lift anyway) in two to three weeks, followed by two weeks at 20 mg. per day, and then none as my own system took control and maintained a happy but controlled hypomania on lithium.

My federal disability retirement has been approved and a return to SSDI is now pending as the salary for which I will create my own job. I could sell my condo here for a profit and move back to my house in Colorado or I could stay in Virginia to write, consult, do patent agenting, work with mental-health "consumer" organizations, and teach a class titled "Living Well with Manic-Depressive Illness."

Sue G. lives in Texas.

My father passed away—he was my friend—two years ago. My lover left me after five years. I got so depressed I could not function, cried constantly, drank a lot, lost twenty pounds in three weeks, never slept, would fall to pieces if someone spoke to me, and was very short-tempered. I tried to kill myself. (My neighbors broke down the door.) When I thought about it again (I knew this time I would have to do it correctly), I decided I needed help. After talking to my eighteen-year-old son, I turned myself into the psychiatric ward of St. David's Hospital. They put me on Paxil. Other than a hormone pill, I take no other medication. I had never been to a psychiatrist or had any therapy before. I had to do something—I was desperate.

The medication has put me on an even keel. I can handle close to anything now. I am much happier, don't yell constantly, can focus now. My friends stood by me, but we get along a lot better now. I have confidence and self-esteem; I feel good about myself.

I felt nervous for a while after starting the medication (but I was also in the hospital). I was in the hospital for two weeks so, after I got home, I had been on Paxil for several weeks. Side effects have been nausea for about an hour after taking the medication (nothing severe), diarrhea (pretty bad), dry mouth—no anxiety.

I am more at peace. I can sleep. I like sex—I am seeing someone now—and I feel desirable. Paxil changed my whole life. I have more energy. The side effects are worth handling to be able to function as a human being.

I went from one pill a day to one and a half when I fell to pieces and got real upset at work one day. The feeling of helplessness lasted about two days. I had not been like that since I got out of the hospital. The therapist said I should not have to be that way, especially since I was doing so well. I should not feel helpless for more than two or three days. They decided to try half of one pill extra to see how I did. It put me back on track. The nausea and all other symptoms remained the same. I am much more hopeful. I don't want to think about getting off the medication.

I have been on Paxil since March 1994. I have a purpose in life, sex is great, and I am more interested in sex and feel more. I am gaining some of the weight back, though I would rather not do that.

Some people still cannot understand how I could have gotten that depressed. Some feel like I should not depend on the medication to get me through. They mean well and are just looking out for me, but they don't understand. Unless you have been in the psychiatric ward under SP [suicide precaution] where they take everything away from you in fear you may harm yourself, and you are a walking zombie for days, you can't understand. I felt safe in the hospital. I now feel safe outside.

Donna Ronco is a forty-four-year-old wife and mother of two teenage girls from Florida.

My problems began in May of 1994. My husband had an on-the-job accident that resulted in a herniated disk. Ninety percent of all people with herniated disks recover within four weeks of the injury by being inactive or performing sedentary work. My husband, unfortunately, fell into the 10 percent who need an operation.

My husband spent six weeks in tremendous pain before the operation was scheduled. We went through days where he could not get out of bed, days where a trip to the bathroom meant crawling in and out (a good thirty-minute round-trip). I found myself having to be Superwoman.

The normal activities of two teenage daughters were limited, because I depended on them to help take care of their father when I was at work. They understood that he was in pain, but this was summer and there were fun-filled days to spend with their friends, swimming, hanging out, and attending amusement parks. These activities required transportation, since neither of them was old enough to drive herself. I couldn't tell them no, because it was their time off from school and I wanted their lives to be as normal as I could make them.

All these factors resulted in my working an eight-hour day at my regular job, then coming home to the job of being mother, driver, wife, nursing aide, and motivator for six long weeks.

During the fourth week I began to realize that I was burning out. I had thrown myself into this role with such vigor that I failed to take care of me. By the fifth week I was really feeling down. My husband realized that I was moody, short-tempered, sad, and had no energy. At this point he convinced me to go see my doctor.

My doctor did a complete physical. The physical results revealed that my hiatal hernia and my stomach ulcers were acting up, the cysts in both of my breasts had increased significantly in size, my hormone levels were completely out of any kind of normal range, and I was menopausal at the ripe old age of forty-three.

The doctor suggested that my depression could partly be due to my abnormal hormone levels and decided to start me on Provera. She also prescribed 20 mg. of Elavil [generic name: amitriptyline; tricyclic antidepressant] each night at bedtime so that I could get a restful sleep (my husband couldn't sleep with his pain, so he tossed and turned all night).

This worked at first, but after a few weeks I realized that I was having hot flashes during the day and at night. I had bouts of anxiety often during the day, and even woke up in the middle of the night due to stressful dreams. At times I felt suicidal. I don't think I really would have done anything, but the thoughts definitely were there. I had no energy. I would come home from work and sleep twelve to fourteen hours if my schedule permitted. I felt all alone, desperate. I had very low self-esteem. I didn't try to put on makeup. I snapped at the kids and became lax in doing the housekeeping chores. We ate from fast-food drive-ins because I didn't feel like cooking.

Observing my behavior, my husband suggested that I return to the doctor. The doctor decided to take me off Elavil and put me on a new medication for depression—Paxil. I was to take one per day. I began my daily pill on a Friday. By Sunday, I was having some weird effects. My tongue was tingly and partially numb. I realized that when I went to the bathroom, it was taking me ten minutes of sitting and adjusting positions to finally be able to urinate. On Monday, I realized that I could not feel my stomach. I had no sensation of needing to eat or drink. My tongue was more numb, and I couldn't taste my food when I did eat.

I phoned the doctor to discuss these symptoms. At this point she was suspecting the Paxil but just attributed it to known side effects and told me to give it a few more days to see if the symptoms subsided. Up to then, I had never been allergic to any medications. I explained that I had an overnight business trip to another state and wanted her opinion on whether to go or cancel my plans. She thought that I would be all right to travel and okayed the trip.

During the flight I realized that I was having equilibrium problems. If I sat perfectly still and looked straight ahead, bending my head neither up nor down, I could keep from feeling dizzy and nauseated. I could not read the book I had brought on board with me because I felt the same nausea and dizziness. I was glad the flight was only an hour long! I rarely get sick on planes, and this flight was uneventful as far as turbulence or stressful maneuvers are concerned. When I disembarked, I joined my business associates accompanying me on the trip and we all started down an escalator. I became so dizzy that I started to fall forward. Luckily one of my business associates had quick reactions and grabbed me just at the last second. It was then that I knew I was experiencing yet more related symptoms.

The next day I was at a customer site with three of my business associates. During a meeting I realized that I had lost all feeling of my bladder, stomach, and tongue. I was having great difficulty urinating and couldn't care less about eating. My mouth was extremely dry. On a break I phoned my doctor to relay the state of my symptoms. She recommended that I discontinue taking the Paxil and asked me to come see her upon my return. Of course, I had already taken my dosage of Paxil for the day.

After the business meeting ended, we were invited to tour the facility. I told my colleagues that I wasn't feeling well and that I would lie down in the car while they toured the facility. One of them rolled the windows down so I would have some air (it was in the high-eighties that day). While they were gone, it started to rain. Realizing that I was getting wet and deciding that I was a little cool anyway, I rolled the windows up. I didn't realize at this point, but later found out, that I had lost my ability to determine whether I was hot or cold. When my friends returned, I was experiencing severe heat exhaustion and was semiconscious. They rushed me to the emergency room of the local hospital. My blood pressure was very high and my breathing was so shallow that I kept setting off the monitor alarm. After three hours, the emergency-room staff agreed with my doctor that I was having a severe reaction to the Paxil. They prescribed 25 mg. of Meclizine, a motion-sickness medication, to counteract the dizziness and nausea. This medication worked well and carried me through the rest of the trip.

After two days of not taking the Paxil, some of my body functions began to return. Finally, after five days of abstention, I had all my functions back. Needless to say, I will never take Paxil again. My doctor explained that the Paxil seemed to be causing my nerve endings to quit functioning. Since there was no stimulation to my organs, they quit functioning as well. My doctor took an alternate path toward my treatment and prescribed 20 mg. of Elavil in the morning and 20 mg. at bedtime.

My depression kept getting worse over the course of the next few weeks, and my doctor increased the Elavil to 75 mg. at bedtime and 25 mg. in the morning. She also added BuSpar [generic name: buspirone; antianxiety drug]—10 mg. every eight hours. I have now been on these medications for five days and the combination seems to be working. I also have begun hormone treatments and am hoping that in a few weeks I will no longer need the antidepressant and antianxiety medications.

June Scott is a sixty-two-year-old woman who lives on the West Coast.

The counselor said I was chemically out of balance, with one part of my psyche stronger than others, as my thoughts of the past were eating up my thinking and energy. I have a past of therapy and other medications. The decision to take Paxil was only a problem of money. Paxil is expensive and not covered by my insurance. A combination of doctor's advice and my own desperation got me started in December 1993.

The first effect of Paxil was a tremendous relief from depression and the inner thoughts that were so disturbing to me. I was able to think of other things. Life became a little more real and less threatening. I could feel the mood change. Yet I was still very nervous. Instead of thinking about the past, I thought about the future and started too many projects. I tend to have a lot of ideas. I had to slow this tendency down. I do volunteer work now. Housekeeping, my appearance, weight, and finances are about as always—fairly okay.

As usual with any drug I take, the side effects eventually became more noticeable. I had a spell of my arms aching and my fingers and hands tingling, which made me stop Paxil for a week. I was also very nervous, had intestinal pain and stomach cramps, blurred vision, and wild dreams at times. All this may or may not be listed in the *PDR* [*Physicians' Desk Reference*] as side effects of Paxil; they may be something else. Even with all the side effects, Paxil has fewer than other drugs. I'm aiming for no drugs.

I can tolerate half a pill (10 mg.) of Paxil a day. I could stop taking it but I am afraid of my thoughts, and Paxil removes some of the fear. With Paxil, I'm more in control of my thoughts. I know deep problems are not resolved by anything external. But the pain can be lessened.

I am fairly healthy, very nervous, and afraid of people and life. I live day by day. My social life is zero. I want to travel, work, draw, and read.

Aaron Grindon is a twenty-eight-year-old white male from a blue-collar, middle-class family. He lives in the Washington, D.C., area.

When I was twenty years old and in college, I had depression for a year before it was diagnosed. My symptoms included a total withdrawal from all my friends, an increase in appetite, an increase in sleep, many periods of crying, thoughts of hopelessness and of suicide.

After reading about depression in a magazine, I sought and received treatment consisting of therapy and medication. My therapist was excellent and his services were provided free of charge by my college. My psychiatrist prescribed amitriptyline [brand names: Elavil, Endep; tricyclic antidepressant] for over a year but it didn't really help. Finally, I went to another doctor, who put me on Nardil [generic name: phenelzine; monoamine oxidase inhibitor (MAOI) antidepressant]. Within three weeks of starting Nardil, I felt better. I remained on Nardil for six months.

I was twenty-six years old and in my last semester of law school when I began to notice physical and behavioral changes. The symptoms increased in frequency and intensity over a three-month period before I realized that all the symptoms were related and that I had depression. My symptoms included a loss of appetite, a ten-pound weight loss, an inability to sleep through the night, crying for no reason, a loss of interest in sex, and impotence. My symptoms were totally physical. Emotionally, I felt pretty good about my life. I was nervous about the future, but I was happy.

I felt good about my life because so many exciting changes were taking place: I would be graduating cum laude from law school in May; I would be moving from Philadelphia to Washington, D.C., in August; and I would be starting my first job as a lawyer in September. I had lived in Philadelphia for five years and had many good friends who I would miss; I did not really know anyone in Washington, D.C.; I was taking the bar exam in late July; and my first relationship, which lasted four years, had amicably ended.

I was highly functional during my entire depression, regardless of whether or not I was taking medication. I exercised, looked good, went to school and work, maintained my friendships and relationships, and maintained my normal financial management. I feel very lucky that I have remained highly functional during my depressive episodes.

I identified my symptoms as depression after three months. The day I realized I had depression, I called around and made an appointment with a psychiatrist for the next day. I asked the doctor to prescribe Nardil, because it worked the last time I had depression. She agreed that I had depression and prescribed Nardil. My physical symptoms ended in about two weeks, and I felt stable for the next two months, from mid-June through late August.

However, during the week prior to the start of my new job, I began to feel extremely depressed and extremely anxious. I made an appointment to see a psychiatrist in Washington, D.C., who does research on mood disorders. I have learned that not all psychiatrists are qualified to treat depression. I have had to be diligent and aggressive in finding a doctor who is diligent and aggressive in treating depression.

My doctor increased my dosage of Nardil. My depression remained severe, and I had side effects from the medicine, including a twelve-pound weight gain, a bloated feeling, a delay in urination, and anorgasmia. After a month he took me off Nardil. In October—seven months into this depressive episode—my doctor prescribed Paxil and lithium [brand name: Eskalith; mood stabilizer]. Between October and January, my doctor increased my dosage of Paxil. I also took Xanax [generic name: alprazolam; antianxiety drug].

After I started taking Paxil, I noticed some side effects, including vivid dreams, morning lethargy, and sweating during the night. The vivid dreams occurred almost every night. Usually only my legs were sweaty when I slept.

After five months on Paxil, I went from having a chronic severe depression to having a chronic low-level depression. A year into this depressive episode, my doctor prescribed Wellbutrin [generic name: bupropion; unicyclic antidepressant] in addition to the Paxil and lithium. With these medications, I experienced side effects—dry mouth, constipation, and loss of appetite—that went away after about one month. I still occasionally have vivid dreams. Once I started Wellbutrin, I no longer sweated during the night.

This combination of medicines worked. My depression ended just a few days later. It was not a gradual ending. It was like flipping a light switch. One morning I woke up and knew that my depression was over. I can't truly describe how I knew that I was better. It was a feeling within me. When you suffer from depression, you become extremely aware of your moods and emotions and what influences them.

I have been feeling better now for about four months. I have energy and motivation. I still have ups and downs. However, the downs are not as deep and are not as long as they were when I was depressed.

Looking back over my life, I know that I also had depression when I was ten years old. I also know that I had several minor depressions between the ages of twenty-one and twenty-six. I know my depression is biological and triggered by major life changes. I will probably be on medication for the rest of my life, but that does not matter. My depression is not a mental illness, but a physical illness that manifests itself in my moods.

Susannah Newport lives in Missouri with her children and husband.

In the fall of 1992, I was diagnosed with chronic low-grade depression. This diagnosis came after sixteen years of intermittent therapy (some as few as two sessions, two as long as eighteen months). No one had ever suggested depression, even though I had struggled to function most of my life. Because I managed to keep my head above water and demonstrated some success (my parenting, my master's degree, my career), I was not diagnosed.

I have lived with this depression since I was six years old. Living was like treading water, and when I got tired from the effort, I would have outbursts of crying, rage, despair, and suicidal thoughts. I attempted suicide once at thirteen, but hid it from people.

I had difficulty concentrating, had low self-esteem, and entered into several emotionally abusive relationships. I had irrational fears that left me feeling frozen. I had constant conversations in my head. I often felt as though my life was only an illusion and that I did not really exist.

When first diagnosed, I was prescribed imipramine [brand names: Tofranil, Janimine; tricyclic antidepressant] and immediately felt a difference. I developed a rash and was taken off the medicine. I had to be off medication for five days to get the imipramine out of my system. During that time I had withdrawal symptoms and felt as though I would fall apart. I took a low dose of an antihistamine to take the edge off of my feelings. The few friends that knew about my depression were very supportive.

I was next prescribed Zoloft. Within days, I knew that something was wrong. Though I was told that they were not common symptoms, jitteriness and a general feeling of being out of sorts, paranoia and panic joined all together in me. My psychiatrist attributed these symptoms to my depression, but having lived with my depression for many years, I knew it was related to the medicine. I was taken off the Zoloft (and had to undergo another period of withdrawal) and switched to Tofranil. Because it was the generic imipramine that previously gave me a rash, there was hope the brand-name drug would be more tolerable.

Tofranil seemed to work fine. Life seemed more manageable. I cried less and was more consistent and positive with my children. The one thing I missed on this medication was dreaming. I also had late-night insomnia (4:00–5:30 A.M.). During this time I entered into a long-distance relationship. I am convinced that it was the support of the medication that allowed me to feel at ease enough to build this relationship, to believe in myself enough.

In February 1993 I became engaged. We discussed the possibility of having children and decided to explore the idea. I was told I could not get pregnant on the medication. After much thought, I decided to switch from Tofranil to homeopathic remedies, with the help of my chiropractor and psychiatrist.

The winter of 1994 brought many changes to my life. I moved to a new house, and my fiancé moved in with me and my three daughters. My ex-husband left town and so was no longer available to participate in the parenting. I was also in intensive therapy, dealing with my incest and abuse issues.

In April I suddenly found myself screaming at the whole staff at work. I behaved very inappropriately. I realized that I had slipped back into my old depression. It snuck up on me and suddenly I felt completely out of control. My boss assigned me to a thirty-day sick leave. It was one of the most frightening experiences of my adult life.

My psychiatrist prescribed Paxil. Since then my life has changed enormously. I lost my job of nine years, got married, and started my own at-home business. My psychiatrist has also added a second medication, BuSpar [generic name: buspirone; antianxiety drug], to help with some of my anxiety.

I don't like the thought of daily medication, and I have trouble remembering my lunch and bedtime doses. I don't like the stigma related to my disorder and sometimes feel sad about my diagnosis.

What I like is that life is easier. I cry at more appropriate times. I feel more at ease with social relationships. I'm a calmer parent (as my children will attest). I have not felt panicked or detached from my life for months. With the support of medication, I am better able to enjoy the progress that I'm making in therapy and in my recovery. I have fingernails most of the time. Medication doesn't take away my problems. I still have some symptoms of post–traumatic stress syndrome, but I have much more than I could have dreamed. I am happy.

Roger Miles lives in Virginia.

I suffer from a nervous condition brought on by the stresses of a remote assignment in Libya with the U.S. Air Force from February 1968 to May 1969. During this period I felt trapped (I couldn't leave the country if I wanted to) and was under the care of an air force psychiatrist. Added to the stress of being a long way from home, I worked long hours in an office and on the flight line and worked for a dictatorial boss. During one evening while serving as officer of the day and reviewing Red Cross messages from the United States requesting that certain airmen return to the States for a severely ill or dying (or dead) family member, I suffered a severe anxiety attack and went to the base hospital, where the doctor on duty gave me an injection of liquid Valium. As a civilian in 1971 I went to the Veterans Administration Hospital in Miami and was diagnosed as having a service-incurred ailment, for which I was awarded a 10 percent disability rating and currently receive a monthly disability check.

During the latter half of 1992 I noticed that my general anxiety level was increasing, and I found myself worrying about my general health. Nothing dramatic was happening in my life to account for this increased anxiety. I have been a runner for years and have been enjoying excellent health, but I started to worry about some upper chest pain (especially when under stress) and visited my primary-care physician at my health maintenance organization in July 1993. He examined me thoroughly, did an ECG and blood work, pronounced me (and my heart) in good condition, and prescribed lorazepam [brand name: Ativan; antianxiety drug]—one or two 5 mg. tablets per day as needed.

I took them when under stress but soon ran out of medication. So I returned to my HMO, only to find the doctor who had prescribed the Ativan was gone. In his place was another physician, who examined me briefly, wrote me another prescription for lorazepam, and referred me to the mental-health department of my HMO in Washington, D.C. Taking one or two Ativan in the morning helped with mounting daily anxiety, but after their effect wore off, the anxiety would return and I would usually have to take a third tablet.

The first psychiatrist that I saw kept me on the Ativan, but since he saw some underlying depression that was the cause of my restless sleep, he prescribed Prozac. The first and only Prozac tablet I took was on a terribly cold day in January 1994, and it caused me such anxiety that I was pacing the floor of my condo, unable to even sit down for more than five minutes. I then called my HMO (it was a Saturday) and spoke with the psychiatrist on duty, who telephoned a prescription for Inderal [generic name: propranolol; antihypertensive] to my local pharmacy. I picked up the Inderal (anxious as I was) and, to my dismay, it had no immediate effect. Still pacing the floor, I was seriously thinking about going to a local hospital emergency room, but decided against it because of the severe cold weather. I subsequently took two tablets of lorazepam, which stopped the anxiety. I fell asleep and when I awoke I felt much better.

Later I related this experience to the clinical psychologist whom I was seeing for work and social problems (mostly my inability to make real friends in the unfriendly Washington,

D.C., area). He called the psychiatrist who had prescribed the Prozac, was given the runaround by that doctor, then suggested another psychiatrist with whom he worked on a daily basis and made me an appointment. My therapist also recorded a relaxation tape, which I played at home mostly in the morning, and it did help some.

When I met with the new psychiatrist, I elaborated my general mental health and what prescription drugs I had been taking, and she prescribed Sinequan [generic name: doxepin; tricyclic antidepressant]. I took less than half a 10 mg. tablet, which made me very sleepy most of the day. The psychiatrist said that it was obvious that the Sinequan was too strong for me and then prescribed Paxil in 20 mg. tablets, saying that it had worked wonders for her other patients.

So I took the Paxil, starting at 10 mg. a day, breaking the 20 mg. tablets in two. The first side effect that the Paxil produced was sweating (mostly on the palms of my hands). But then on Easter Sunday, while over at my mother's apartment, I started experiencing chest pains, along with some sweating. The symptoms subsided as the day wore on, but I was quite anxious (as was my mother), yet I was reluctant to take the Valium that she offered. I called the doctor on Monday morning after an almost sleepless night, and she said that the symptoms I was experiencing were nothing to be alarmed at but that I should have taken the Valium for the anxiety.

Still concerned about the chest pains, I called my physician and described my symptoms. Although she was skeptical that the chest pains were heart-related, she nevertheless authorized a treadmill ECG. So I took the test at a local cardiologist's office and was delighted to find out that my heart is in fine shape.

When I take Paxil daily and in the recommended dosage, I find that it produces a mellowing effect. In fact, it can put me to sleep if I'm relaxing at home. It minimizes the anxiety that I've also been having problems with, and I can get through my working day easier. Moreover, once my body got used to Paxil, the drug has produced hardly any side effects. It helps me sleep through the night and hasn't interfered with my driving.

Elizabeth Kirby resides in Colorado.

I have suffered from depression for about fifteen years on and off. I have used tricyclic antidepressants during that period. I have a college degree in economics and obtained my nursing license in 1981. I've worked in the field of mental health and drug and alcohol rehabilitation for nine years.

Three years ago I began to have problems concentrating, remembering, and thinking clearly. I was embarrassed and felt stupid and was emotionally labile. I was started on a course of Elavil [generic name: amitriptyline; tricyclic antidepressant], 150 mg. at bedtime, and Tegretol [generic name: carbamazepine; anticonvulsant], 200 mg. at bedtime. These weren't very helpful in alleviating the symptoms but made life passable. I had several mornings where I didn't wake up for work but was excused when I had a person from a program for impaired nurses explain my depression and medication. During this time I also experienced some moments or days that were euphoric and everything was great.

My four-year relationship began to suffer, as did my two children, ages eleven and twelve. My depression got deeper and more lengthy, and my euphoric episodes increased. I began therapy once again and was tried on a myriad of medications and combinations of them. I began seeing a psychiatrist who finally diagnosed manic-depression, and I was begun on lithium [brand names: Lithane, Carbolith; mood stabilizer], along with the Elavil and Tegretol. I saw her three times per week. My job was transferred to another site and I was unable to keep up a normal facade. I took a medical leave in January 1993 and haven't worked since.

I was hospitalized in February and in May 1993 for ECT [electroconvulsive therapy]. ECT made my memory much worse, and it caused nightmares and paranoia. By this time I was on SSDI [Social Security disability insurance], with no medical benefits, so I couldn't do therapy. I worked with my family doctor, and still do, and I asked her if we could try Paxil, starting March 1994.

About three to four weeks after I began to take Paxil, I began to feel different—very different—but I was afraid to say anything to anyone in case it wasn't true. Finally, at six weeks it was noticeable. I could wake up, get up, and I felt good! I began to do things and follow through. I cared about my appearance and spent more quality time with my kids, now sixteen and seventeen.

My dose is now at 50 mg. (I still take Elavil and Tegretol), and although I don't feel as great as I did initially, I can do things, make plans, work with vocational rehab, and entertain the idea of returning to work. My kids are both back home—they had been placed in group homes as I couldn't care for them.

In short, Paxil is the first antidepressant to work for me, and dramatically so. The side effects have been: increased dry mouth and throat, some diarrhea, blurry vision, and—the only that is truly uncomfortable—periods of sudden, profuse sweating. Even with the last side effect, I consider Paxil a godsend and do not intend to stop taking it. (It helps that I qualify for free Paxil from the pharmaceutical company because I have no medical coverage. On average, Paxil costs me $140 per month.) My state of mental and physical health is 75 percent better, and I know it is, without a doubt, the combination of Paxil and the other meds. Having Paxil work was like being lifted out of quicksand.

Serah Jackson is nineteen years old and lives in Wisconsin.

My family history is one that seems very common these days, but I feel it has played a unique part in my depression and eventual decision to be placed on medication. My father was in Laos and Vietnam in 1970–71. From what I understand, he came back with pretty severe PTSD [post–traumatic stress disorder] and an addiction to smack. He and my mother were married a couple years later, and I was born on July 10, 1975. My sister was born in 1978. I guess my mom and dad weren't really happy together; they ended up divorcing when I was seven.

I remember that day as clear as if it were today. I was in second grade, and I came home to find my dad packing up his personal items. I listened to them fight over who got what dishes. I had no idea what was happening; all I could figure out in my mind was that Daddy didn't love us anymore and was leaving. I guess that was the beginning of my deep-seated fear of abandonment. After the divorce things went downhill very fast. My mom, over the course of time, became severely dependent on both alcohol and cocaine. I, on the other hand, used food to numb my fears. Looking back, I see it was the only consistent thing I seemed to have. We always had food.

Since I am the oldest, I jumped right into the mode of caretaker with very little difficulty. I always made it my duty to take care of our little family. I was so busy being a mother to my mom that I pretty much missed out on any piece of a normal childhood. My mom got remarried when I was about eight; my dad, when I was nine. With my mom's remarriage, I got a stepdad and two stepbrothers, one older and one younger. I guess I must have been about twelve or thirteen when my older stepbrother began to sexually abuse me. To avoid making myself sick while writing this, I'll just say he did almost everything but rape me. This went on for approximately three to four years. I can't place it exactly; a lot of it I don't remember wholly, just fragments.

After many unsuccessful solo attempts to stop using chemicals, my mom went into treatment when I was about fourteen. As well as being a big turning point in her life, it was a big change for me, too. All of a sudden I had this mother who cooked and cleaned and was a regular Donna Reed. This is what I feel triggered the beginning of my continuous struggle with depression. I felt like I wasn't needed anymore; there was nobody left for me to take care of. I became incredibly withdrawn, isolated myself from the few friends I had, and ate more than ever. Looking back, I notice the biggest increase in my weight was during this period.

I expressed my frequent thoughts of death and dying to anyone who would listen. I was a little girl trapped in an adult's body. I clearly remember, after one of the first times I told anyone about my suicidal thoughts, being taken to see some counselor. I was then placed in an inpatient treatment facility for adolescents dealing with depression. I spent thirty days there and honestly thought I was cured, only to realize a year down the road that those same feelings had popped up again and had gained intensity. This time I became self-abusive, burning my wrists, etc. I was placed in another treatment center to try and fix me. It was about this time they began using medications to try and ease the depression.

The first antidepressant I ever took was Prozac. It was right about the time it became so popular, and both my parents and my psychiatrist thought it was a great idea. The only part of this whole deal that seemed to involve me was that I had to remember to take the stuff. I was not involved in the decision to try an antidepressant at all. I took Prozac faithfully for about a year with no major side effects, besides having difficulty sleeping.

After that first year, I still took it as loyally as ever, believing that it was a miracle drug like everyone said it was. I felt like a totally new me was emerging. I didn't want to die, had energy and the whole "I'm getting better" thing. I felt like I was a such a success story until about six months later. The suicidal thoughts all came back, but with a greater intensity and seriousness. I abused myself worse than I ever had before—I still bear the scars to this day. I blame Prozac, this supposed miracle drug, for a lot of the physical pain I subjected myself to. This is only my story, but I feel it is evidence enough.

The next antidepressant I took was Wellbutrin [generic name: bupropion; unicyclic antidepressant]. This seemed to work satisfactorily, with a headache the only noticeable side effect after I took the second dose.

I can't explain why, but once again I tried Prozac, this time in combination with trazodone [brand name: Desyrel; serotonin agonist] to help me sleep. It did just the opposite. I became unable to sleep at all and I was in a zombielike state. I spoke with my doctor about this reaction, and we decided to stop both medications.

I wasn't on any antidepressants from age sixteen until about February of 1994. I can't say that I was as depressed as before during this period, but my quality of life was very poor and I was not as happy as I feel I could have been. In February 1994, I started Paxil. I began at 20 mg. per day and ended up at

40 mg. Of all the drugs I have taken for my depression, I feel this has worked the best. I felt results in about one week, which was just amazing. I had energy, had no suicidal thoughts, everything was going very well.

Actually, it's only about one week ago that I stopped taking Paxil. Lately I have been having very intrusive, consuming thoughts that I need to die. It's not a distinct voice, but I feel there is something or someone telling me this. I can't sleep—I just lie in bed waiting for sleep to come. I spoke with my psychiatrist about this and she wanted to try me on nortriptyline [brand names: Pamelor, Aventyl; tricyclic antidepressant], along with a sleeping pill on an as-needed basis.

I felt effects from this drug the day following my first dosage. I felt very dizzy and disoriented. I was unable to sleep. (I elected not to take the sleeping pills to make sure it was the nortriptyline doing this and not the sleeping pills.) In general, I had a feeling similar to a hangover but more intense. I feel much more lethargic and much more suicidal on this medication than without it. I stopped taking it three days ago, and I'm still feeling very dizzy and somewhat nauseated. It's my belief that an antidepressant should help you function better, not debilitate you. I have elected not to take nortriptyline anymore, and will seriously consider any and all possible side effects before taking another antidepressant.

Appendix: Guidelines for Writing a Personal Account for the *Living with* Series

The purpose of the entire *Living with* series is to present what people experience when using antidepressant drugs or treatment. Each book gathers together first-person accounts in a readable paperback format.

The second book in the series, due in 1996 after *Living with Prozac and Other SSRIs,* is *Living with Tricyclic Antidepressants (TCAs)*. TCAs—the largest class of antidepressants (and I'm including here unicyclic and heterocyclic drugs)—are used, like SSRIs, to treat a large variety of conditions.

I plan to compile two additional volumes in the series:

Living with Electroconvulsive Therapy (ECT)—although most people are unaware of it, ECT is one of the most frequently used treatments for depression in psychiatric hospitals today.

Living with Lithium—this crystalline salt, more correctly called lithium carbonate, is widely prescribed for short- and long-term treatment of bipolar disorder (manic-depression) and treatment-resistant depression.

The following guidelines were used in the writing of all accounts for *Living with Prozac and Other SSRIs*. The guidelines were designed to structure each account to be as subjective, straightforward, and appropriate as possible.

Imagine you are telling a story to a friend with whom you want to share your experience. See this as an exercise in expressing your whole attitude and history with medications. Write a narrative approximately two to four pages, typed and double-spaced. Remember the "friend" who is "hearing" this story wants to learn all about the medication so as to be a better friend as well as to be an educated patient, should this person ever undergo a similar condition or illness. You may choose to tell your story chronologically or to tailor the narrative to explore specific emotion(s) or issue(s).

Write about your condition before you went on medication: what you felt and how you behaved; how you differed from your previous or usual self. What circumstances were there, if any, that may have aggravated the already existing (normal) problems you had? We want to know the context for the decision you made to take antidepressant medication. Were you depressed? If not, please discuss your diagnosed or diagnosable condition. How did (or didn't) you function in your life (including work, social or volunteer activities, parenting, romantic/sex life, housecleaning, and personal care—your appearance, weight, financial management, the state of your car [if applicable])?

Write about the decision to take medication: which medication(s) was (were) first suggested by your therapist, psychiatrist, or doctor and discussed with you? What helped you make your decision (information a doctor gave you; a loved one's advice; your own desperation [these are only suggestions]) to take medication?

Write about the effects you felt when you were first taking medication, even if there were or seemed to be none (everything is of interest here, nothing is irrelevant). Were (or are) you feeling better? What does "better" mean to you? What does "better" mean to your family/loved ones? How did the medication help you in dealing with your closest friends or family members, your social situations, your work, your daily tasks, your past, your self-image, your depression or other condition?

Were (or are) you aware of side effects? Did (do) you feel jittery? More at peace? Could (can) you sleep at night? Did you have (or are you having) any changes to your sexual life—your responses or desires? Please answer explicitly but appropriately. How are these effects different from the changes your condition (or illness) created? Did you have (or are you having) more or less energy, headaches, digestive problems (nausea/bloating/diarrhea/constipation), dry mouth, sweats, anxiety at night or during the day?

Have you or your doctor(s) changed your medication(s)? Why? What has that meant to you—physically (less nausea? more lethargy?) or emotionally (Are you more hopeful? Are you discouraged?)? If you are off medication, how are you different?

Write about all the effects you felt after a few weeks; after a few months; after, if applicable, six to eight months; a year; more than one or two years. How did you (or do you) function in your life (including work, social or volunteer activities, parenting, romantic/sex life, housecleaning, and personal care—your appearance, weight, financial management, the state of your car [if applicable])?

How would you describe your state of health and/or mind now? How has (have) your medication(s) affected your health and/or mind(set)?

These are guidelines to offer direction and to remind you of the finer points of your story. There is no wrong way to write your contribution.

Select Bibliography

Bezchlibnyk-Butler, Kalyna, et al., eds. *Clinical Handbook of Psychotropic Drugs.* Seattle, WA: Hogrefe & Huber Publishers, 1994.

Bloomfeld, Harold H., M.D., and Peter McWilliams. *How to Heal Depression.* Los Angeles, CA: Prelude Press, 1994.

Breggin, Peter R., M.D. *Talking Back to Prozac.* New York: St. Martin's Press, 1994.

Cronkite, Kathy. *On the Edge of Darkness: Conversations About Conquering Depression.* New York: Doubleday, 1994.

Duke, Patty, with Gloria Hochman. *A Brilliant Madness: Living with Manic-Depressive Illness.* New York: Bantam Books, 1992.

Fieve, Ronald R., M.D. *Prozac.* New York: Avon Books, 1994.

Guttmacher, Laurence B., M.D. *Concise Guide to Psychopharmacology and Electroconvulsive Therapy.* Washington, DC: American Psychiatric Press, Inc., 1994.

Jack, Dana Crowley. *Silencing the Self: Women and Depression.* New York: HarperPerennial, 1993 (paperback); Boston, MA: Harvard University Press, 1991.

Keltner, Norman L., Ed.D., R.N., and David G. Folks, M.D. *Psychotropic Drugs.* St. Louis, MO: Mosby-Year Book, Inc., 1993.

Kramer, Peter D., M.D. *Listening to Prozac: A Psychiatrist Explores Antidepressant Drugs and the Remaking of the Self.* New York: Penguin Books, 1994 (paperback); New York: Viking Penguin, 1993.

McCoy, Kathleen. *Coping with Teenage Depression: A Parent's Guide*. New York: New American Library, 1982.

Manning, Martha. *Undercurrents: A Therapist's Reckoning with Her Own Depression*. San Francisco: HarperSanFrancisco, 1995.

Millett, Kate. *The Loony-Bin Trip*. New York: Simon & Schuster, 1990.

Mondimore, Francis M., M.D. *Depression: The Mood Disease*. Baltimore, MD: Johns Hopkins University Press, 1990.

Papolos, Demitri, F., M.D., and Janice Papolos. *Overcoming Depression*. New York: Harper & Row, 1987.

Shreeve, Caroline, M.D. *Overcoming Depression: Its Causes and How to Overcome It*. New York: Harper & Row, 1985 (paperback); London: Thorsons, 1984.

Silverman, Harold M., et. al. *The Pill Book* (annual). New York: Bantam Books.

Styron, William. *Darkness Visible: A Memoir of Madness*. New York: Random House, 1991.

Thorne, Julia. *You Are Not Alone: Words of Experience and Hope for the Journey Through Depression*. New York: HarperPerennial, 1993.

Wolman, Benjamin B., ed. *Depressive Disorders: Facts, Theories, and Treatment Methods*. New York: John Wiley & Sons, Inc., 1990.

Wurtzel, Elizabeth. *Prozac Nation: Young and Depressed in America*. Boston, MA: Houghton Mifflin, 1994.

General Index

Drug Index